2005

# Cooking in the Moment

Four seasons of cooking on an island in Maine

*Kyra Alex*

Published by Short Circuit Press
P.O. Box 458
Deer Isle, Maine  04627
email: shortcircuitpress@yahoo.com

Design by Zoë Alexis Scott, Short Circuit Press.


Printing by Thompson-Shore, Salinas, Michigan.

ISBN: 0-9773986-0-8

This book is dedicated to
Laurie Klemenz
and
Nichole Hammett

# "Thanks for the Ding Dong ..." Bruce Greenlaw

## ~ Acknowledgements ~

Editing: Ethel Clifford, Renee Sewall and Judy Rader

Graphic design and quality inspiration: Zoë Alexis Scott

Cover Painting: Judy Rader

Cover photo: David Klopfenstein

Line drawings: Renee Sewall and Judy Rader


Additional gratitude to:

Renee Sewall for making me realize I didn't have to
write the book in a week;

All of my eager and honest recipe testers;

The island and its people for giving me so many wonderful moments.

# Cooking in the Moment

I'm happy to be able to include gluten-free and surgar-free recipes
for baked items, which can be referenced from the index.

*I love my life.*
*I say that to people all time.*

*It has been almost nine years since I packed up my Kitchen Aid and headed for my dream of living on Deer Isle in Maine. Coming here, I hoped to embrace a community and a way of life that I had romanticized about since childhood. Waking this morning I realized that the community has embraced me. No one could ask for more.*

*How do I wrap up in a few paragraphs what it is like to live and cook on an island in Maine? Every moment here is special for me and each moment seems to be defined by food and the people I share it with. Many of my moments are established by what I will be cooking that day, either at the café or in my own home. My decisions are determined by what the sky looks like, who will be around me, what kinds of chores are on my list. Will it be a crazy day or easy and relaxing? Then I take in the snow or the birds or the dog barking next door and breathe in the moments that define the essence of living here.*

*Island life is so delicately balanced. It is almost impossible to put into words.*

*Friends, neighbors, strangers, customers, helping hands. Unexpected smiles and unexpected tears.*

*Snowy days, starry nights, blue, green and steel gray waters. Birds calling, quilting, pine needle paths.*

*Yard sales, music, plays, celebrations, lives lost. Mobile homes, 10 bedroom mansions, boats, lobsters, weddings, babies, the colors of the sky. ATV'S, burning rubber, politics. Sons and daughters, 5th cousins on both sides, secret places. There is more.*

*Come with me to a baby shower, a summer dinner in a big house, a picnic on a boat, on an island, in a backyard, on a deck. Share in potlucks, gatherings around woodstoves, church suppers, dinner out, dinner in, by the fire, on the screened in porch. Lunch at the café, brunch on Christmas day.*

*Come, have some food, listen to a story or two and let the subtle nuances of life on Deer Isle unfold . . . in the moment.*

*~ Kyra Alex*

# Pantry Essentials

*Cooking in the moment is simple if you have a few staple pantry items always on hand.*
*When buying ingredients always buy the freshest and the best quality that you can afford. This will insure great flavor and great moments.*

A really good all around extra virgin olive oil
( I use Bertolli at work and Athena Greek Olive Oil
at home)

Red wine vinegar

Balsamic vinegar

Sherry vinegar

A good Dijon mustard (Annie's dijon is gluten free
and Martial Picat is a wonderful french Dijon)

French lentils (two popular varieties are
Indigo and Du Puy )

Your favorite dried beans (flageolet are mine)

Sea salt

Kosher salt

Black peppercorns and a grinder

Sun dried tomatoes in oil

Garlic

Onions

Red potatoes

Red and white wine, inexpensive, but good flavor for
cooking. Never use the cooking wines they sell on the
shelf at the grocery store.

Dried porcini mushrooms

A quality jarred tomato sauce

San Marzano canned tomatoes

Chicken broth

All-fruit jam or preserves

Nut butter

Your favorite nuts (mine are pecans and almonds)

## Refrigerator Essentials

Feta cheese (preferably Greek or French for their
creaminess)

Parmesan Reggiano cheese

Eggs (from a local farm if available)

Fresh lemons

Champagne (optional!)

# Winter

*Winter weather on the island varies from year to year. The best winters for me are filled with snow and sunshine. Just this past December we had a wonderful snow storm in the morning and by afternoon it was sunny and 25 degrees. With our snow pants shusshing and our torpedo sleds under our arms, Renee and I joined friends at the country club to do some sliding. I love whizzing down a steep hill on my little plastic sled and I don't know what tires me more, all the laughing we do or those dreadful walks back up the hill.*

# Doughnuts

*Making doughnuts is not as easy as it seems. It took me three years to perfect these and I wasn't really confident I had until the famous doughnut lady herself, Marie McKennan, ate one and told me that they were good. For 30 years, thousands of warm doughnuts were shipped from Marie's kitchen in Stonington to the hungry tummies of her faithful customers. When I moved here in 1997 a stroke had slowed Marie down to just baking for friends and family and I will never forget the day she came in to the café with a brown paper bag filled with her famous doughnuts for me to try. I truly feel honored that mine finally passed the test.*

*P.S. There is another doughnut queen living in Sunshine and she makes the best raised doughnuts I have ever eaten. Lucky for me her granddaughter, Ellen, worked at Lily's for a few years and became a dear friend. The funny part is that Ellen married Mark (Marie's grandson), and neither of them (Mark nor Ellen) can make a doughnut to save their life.*

4 cups unbleached all purpose flour

1 Tbls baking powder

1 Tbls ground nutmeg

1 ½ tsp salt

2 eggs

1 egg yolk

1 cup sugar

1 Tbls pure vanilla extract

4 Tbls melted unsalted butter

1 cup milk

Vegetable or Canola oil for frying

**Makes 15 donuts and 15 holes**

Whisk flour, baking powder, nutmeg and salt together in a large bowl. In another bowl, beat the eggs, yolk, and sugar together until creamy. Add the milk, melted butter and vanilla and beat until smooth.

Mix the wet ingredients into the dry using a rubber spatula. Gently stir until smooth and well combined but don't over mix. Set in refrigerator to chill for 20 minutes to firm up.

Heat oil to 365 degrees. We use a little home fryer that I bought at Sam's some years ago. It regulates the temperature and that is the key to good doughnuts.

Flour your work surface and pat dough ¾ -1 inch thick. Cut doughnuts out with doughnut cutter and fry in batches of three. 1 minute and 13 seconds per side is perfect.

I leave some plain and coat some in cinnamon sugar. (1 cup sugar to 1 Tbls cinnamon)

Serve warm.

# Quick Dough Cinnamon Rolls

*Often people dream of living on the island year round. They spend magical summers in their secluded houses by the sea and move here full time to discover the "simpler" way of life. Unfortunately for many, secluded becomes isolated and simpler becomes stressful. My transition from away to here has been so wonderful that when people began to share these stories of isolation with me I had a hard time relating. But then it dawned on me: I live right on Route 15 and I work in a café. I see people every day. I realized I was taking my tremendous connection with the island and its people for granted. The importance of my winter mornings in the café became crystal clear. Seven different regulars grace my doorstep between 7am and 8am. We discuss movies, politics, hair stylists, the weather, who's getting some and who isn't and whatever else comes to our minds.*

*Bruce tells us all to "be happy in your work" and we all move on into our days feeling that warm embrace of community. These cinnamon rolls are one of their most favorite things to find on the counter to go with their coffee.*

*This recipe makes a big batch. If you are a small batch of people, feel free to cut the recipe in half or put some extras in the freezer for that unexpected visit.*

### For the dough

5 cups unbleached all purpose flour

½ cup sugar

2 ½ tsps baking powder

1 ¼ tsps baking soda

1 tsp salt

12 Tbls unsalted butter, very cold and cut into small pieces

2 ½ cups buttermilk

1 Tbls pure vanilla extract

Preheat oven to 400 degrees.

In a large bowl, stir together the flour, sugar, baking powder, baking soda and salt.

Using a pastry blender or your fingertips, cut the butter into the flour until it is the consistency of coarse cornmeal. Stir in the buttermilk and vanilla until the dough begins to hold together. DO NOT OVERMIX!! Turn the dough out onto a very well floured surface and knead gently until it comes together into a smooth mass. Roll or pat it out to a rectangle that is ½ inch thick.

### For the filling

4 Tbls unsalted butter, melted

Brown sugar

Cinnamon

Walnuts or pecans, coarsely chopped (optional)

Raisins (optional)

Brush butter over the surface of the dough. Then cover with brown sugar, then the cinnamon ( I use a lot) then sprinkle with nuts and raisins if using. (I've put fresh peaches, jam, berries all kinds of things in.)

From the long side begin to roll up jelly roll fashion to form a log.

Cut log into 1-inch-thick rolls and place the rolls on a lightly greased or parchment paper-lined baking tray about an inch apart. Bake rolls until firm to the touch and light golden brown. I use a toothpick to see if the center is cooked through. About 15-20 minutes.

### For the glaze

¼ cup cream

Juice of ½ a lemon

Pinch of pure vanilla extract

2 cups confectioners sugar

Meanwhile, whisk the ingredients for the glaze together until smooth and creamy. Smear each roll with glaze while they are still pretty warm.

### Makes 15-20 depending on how big you cut them

# Smokey Adzuki Bean Dip

*The chill of winter on the island brings with it many evenings curled up on the sofa by the woodstove. I wanted a bean dip that would stand up to a hearty glass of red wine or a good dark beer. This does it. Try it with crusty french bread or your favorite chips. You can substitute French lentils or Jacob Cattle beans, but the Adzuki beans have a wonderful creamy sweetness to them that works very nicely.*

½ pound dried Adzuki beans

4 ounces cream cheese

2 Tbls fresh lemon juice

¼ cup chopped fresh parsley

1 – 2 tsps salt

½ tsp smoked paprika

¼ - ½ tsp chipotle powder

1 ½ tsp sherry or balsamic vinegar

3-4 Tbls olive oil

**Makes 2 cups**

Place the beans in a saucepan and cover by 2 inches with cold water. Bring to a boil, reduce heat and simmer beans until tender, about 1 hour. Add more water as necessary to keep beans covered. Drain and allow beans to cool for 15 minutes.

Place beans and all remaining ingredients, starting with 1 teaspoon of salt and the ¼ tsp chipotle powder, in the bowl of a food processor. Process dip until creamy. You can make it smooth or leave small pieces of bean, your choice. Add more salt and chipotle powder to taste

I have served this along side roasted halibut as a quick and delicious sauce.

VARIATION
For a summer dip, use navy beans. Add 3 cloves of fresh garlic. Omit the smoked paprika and chipotle powder. Skip the vinegar and add more lemon juice.

# Velvet Flageolet Bean Soup
## with rosemary & garlic

*The classic question to year round people from summer people is "what do you do here all winter?"*

*I am sure many of you know the classic answer, "@#$% and make babies". While that may be true, there are many other ways to entertain oneself. One brilliant idea I had was to start a book club. I put a note up at the café inviting anyone to join and ended up with about 8 interested readers. At about the same time I discovered this wonderful bean called flageolet. Of course I was drawn to its name by the similarity to flatulence and the result for most of us after eating beans. The reality is that they are from France, they are beautiful hues of pale green and white and they have the most velvet texture of any cooked dried bean I have ever encountered. In fact, after some research I found them to be called the Cadillac of beans.*

*Anyway, the book club started off with a bang, passionate opinions, self declarations, even some tears of compassion. I made this soup one night and gave everyone a bag of beans to take home. It couldn't have been better.*

*Unfortunately the book club ended after a year, kind of like a big old bean fart, but the soup lives on.*

3 cups of Flageolet beans

2 Tbls olive oil

2 large yellow onions, chopped

8 cloves of garlic, chopped

8 cups of chicken stock

1 tsp dried rosemary, or to taste

Salt and pepper

½ cup sliced scallions

extra virgin olive oil

**Serves 6 to 8**

Heat 2 tablespoons of olive oil in a large soup pot over medium heat. Add onion and garlic and saute until golden. Stir in beans and pour in stock. Add salt to taste.

Simmer beans partially covered until very tender, approximately 1 hour. Add more stock if necessary to keep beans covered in liquid by ½ inch. When beans are tender, puree until smooth and velvety. Adjust seasoning with salt and pepper.

Serve with scallions, fresh rosemary if you have any and drizzle with a good fruity olive oil.

Delicious!

# Warm Lentil Salad with Goat Cheese

*Okay, every so often you need to get off the island. It clears your head and reminds you of why you love the island so much. This is a version of a delicious lentil salad I had at Prune in New York City.*

### Lentils

2 cups Beluga or De Puy lentils

6 cups cold water

4-6 cloves garlic, cut in half

2 fresh sage leaves

2 sprigs parsley

1 bay leaf

1 Tbls sea salt

2 ounce piece of pancetta (optional)

⅓ cup olive oil

1 dried chipotle pepper, seeds removed

Place lentils in a pot and cover with water. Add remaining flavor ingredients – if you have cheese cloth you can make a pouch to hold all the flavor ingredients, making it easier to remove after cooking. I usually just throw them in the pot and pick them out when I drain the lentils-. Bring water to boil, reduce heat to a gentle simmer and cook lentils 'til al dente, 20-25 minutes. Drain lentils and remove all other ingredients.

### Vinaigrette dressing

2 Tbls balsamic vinegar

2 Tbls chopped fresh parsley

1 tsp Dijon mustard

Salt and pepper to taste

½ cup or to taste, fruity olive oil

Whisk all ingredients except oil in a bowl to combine. Whisk oil into bowl in a slow, steady stream until completely combined. You can also do this in a small bowl of a food processor, running the machine as you stream in the oil. Taste and adjust seasoning with salt and pepper.

### Serves 6

### Salad

¼ - ½ pound of fresh salad greens
(Fresh mesclun if available)

I bunch scallions, chopped

I pint sun gold tomatoes, halved

I red or yellow pepper, seeded and
diced

4 ounces creamy feta cheese ( Greek
or French is the best) crumbled

Toss warm lentils in a ¼ cup of vinaigrette dressing. Heap dressed lentils on salad greens. Top with scallions, tomatoes, pepper and feta. Serve extra dressing on the side.

Makes enough for 4-6 main course salads or 8-10 side servings

VARIATION
I often add sliced cooked chicken breast to the salad when I have it to make it a very hardy meal.

# Pan Fried Potatoes

*Oddly enough it has taken me years to perfect this simple dish, but now that I have, you can't beat it.*
*These are great in the morning with eggs, in the evening with sausage or at lunch by themselves with whatever*
*leftovers you have in the fridge tossed in at the end.  Oh, and in the summer, try them with sharp cheddar cheese,*
*garden tomatoes and fresh basil — to die for.*

4 medium red potatoes (you can use any type of potato, but these come out the creamiest in the center)

½ cup onion, roughly chopped ( the sweet long red onions available here in the summer are awesome)

4 Tbls olive oil

Kosher salt to taste

**Serves 6**

Cut potatoes into fairly uniform ¾-inch pieces.

Place them in a 10" cast iron skillet.  Sprinkle liberally with salt and 1 tablespoon olive oil.

Turn burner on low and cover potatoes. Turning occasionally, cook covered until just tender.

Remove cover and turn heat to medium high.  Cook potatoes until beginning to get golden brown. Toss onions into pan and adjust with salt.  Continue to cook until potatoes are crispy and deep brown and onions are tender and carmelized, this takes about 25 minutes.  Don't stir too often, let the potatoes have time to brown.

Eat now, or add anything you want to them.

VARIATION
Nichole and I fight over these when I have avocados on hand.
Use sweet potatoes instead of red potatoes, cook using the same method, but season lightly with rosemary.
At the end, stir in a diced avocado and pieces of cooked chicken. Serve with sour cream.

# Broccoli Sautéed in Olive Oil with Garlic

*The produce selection on the island in the winter is a bit limited. We eat a lot of broccoli. This method is delicious with other vegetables like green beans too. Add any spices that you desire.*

1 head of broccoli, cut into florets. (When I am cooking, I leave quite a bit of stem on. When Renee makes this she removes most of the stem,. You decide)

Water

2 Tbls olive oil

2 cloves of garlic, sliced

Salt and Pepper to taste

**Serves 6**

Place broccoli florets in heavy bottom skillet and add a ¼ inch of water.

Sprinkle with a bit of sea salt.

Cover and simmer until broccoli is almost tender.

Drain water and place skillet back over medium high heat without the cover. Let all the water evaporate and add the oil and garlic. Season with salt and saute broccoli until tender.

# Pan Seared Scallops with Pancetta & Peas

*When I first moved here the owner of an historic Inn had me to tea to try to help me get acclimated to the area. She told me that scallops were in season here in the dead of winter and the Inn bought hundreds of pounds to freeze and serve in the summer. Where was I going to put hundreds of pounds of scallops? For a few years I did buy 60 pounds or so and froze them successfully. Unfortunately I would forget they were in the freezer during the crazy busy summer and would be trying to eat them all in the fall before the season started again. Now, I still buy lots of scallops in the winter, but we feature them on the menu while the snow is on the ground. By November we are all craving the first batch of the season.*

1 pound fresh sea scallops

4 ounces Pancetta or bacon, cut into small diced pieces

1 clove garlic, chopped

1 tsp grated fresh ginger

¼ cup sherry

2 cups stock

1 cup cream  (I substitute unsweetened soy milk in this dish very successfully)

1 cup fresh or frozen peas

Tabasco to taste

2 Tbls chopped fresh parsley

Salt and pepper

**Serves 4-6**

Cook Pancetta in a heavy- bottomed skillet, not non-stick. Render fat and cook until crispy and browned. With a slotted spoon, remove the bacon and leave 2 tablespoons of fat in the skillet.

Over high heat, add scallops in batches, don't over-crowd or they won't brown nicely. Sear both sides until deep golden brown, about 1 ½ minutes per side.  (Don't over-cook scallops, you want them soft in the middle. Remove scallops to a plate while making the pan sauce.) Stir garlic into hot skillet, cook 30 seconds. Add sherry, bring to boil and reduce by half. Add stock, bring back to a boil, add peas and cook until just tender and stock reduces by ½, about 3 minutes. Add cream and boil until thickened.

Stir in bacon, parsley and Tabasco sauce. If scallops have cooled, place them back in pan and reheat in sauce. Or just serve sauce over wam scallops. This is delicious over mashed potatoes.

VARIATION
Sprinkle the scallops lightly with cayenne pepper. Cook bacon and sear scallops in fat with ¼ cup diced sun dried tomatoes. Remove scallops. Add garlic. Add white wine instead of sherry and use one (14-oz.) can diced tomatoes with juice instead of stock. Add peas and ¼ cup diced Kalamata olives with tomatoes. Simmer until thickened, 5-10 minutes. Stir in parsley and bacon, omitting cream and Tabasco. Season with salt and pepper. Delicious over polenta.

# Baked Fish with a Brown Butter Caper Sauce

*This simple sauce will turn your humble kitchen into a 5 star restaurant. Use any type of mild white fish. Halibut is my favorite.*

1 ½ pounds fresh white fish, cut into
4 six ounce servings

Olive oil

Juice of ½ a lemon

8 Tbls unsalted butter

1 Tbls balsamic vinegar

2 Tbls jarred capers

**Serves 4**

Preheat oven to 400 degrees.

Drizzle fish with olive oil and sprinkle with lemon juice. Bake in oven until just firm in the center, about 10 – 15 minutes.

Meanwhile, in a heavy-bottomed skillet, melt butter. Let the melted butter continue to cook in the skillet until it just starts to turn golden brown. Watch it carefully because it doesn't take too much time to burn the butter. When the butter is golden, carefully add the balsamic vinegar. It will sputter a bit.

Add capers and heat through. Pour over warm fish and serve immediately.

# Whole Butterflied Chicken Roasted
## over fresh vegetables

*A few times a month in the winter I feature Cooking 101 in the kitchen at the café. The classes are small and the people are always eager to learn. After all the chopping, stirring and dicing we gather in the dining room and eat what we have made. It is fun to talk about food and to get to know people from the inside of the kitchen rather than just from the opposite side of the counter. This version of roasted chicken is always quite popular and really makes handling a whole chicken a breeze. You cut out the backbone and lay the chicken flat over whatever vegetables you want to roast under it. I bumped into a fellow at a farmers market buying leeks. He said he roasted the leeks under his chicken and threw the chicken out. I totally understood what he meant. Butterflying it makes it easy to stuff things up under the skin too, like herbs and oils, etc., and carving it is a breeze.*

1 whole chicken, rinsed and patted dry

1 bunch of baby leeks, white and pale green parts only, or 1 sweet onion, peeled and cut into ¼-inch slices

1 bunch of baby carrots, peeled

4-5 cloves of garlic

A bunch of your favorite fresh herbs (I like parsley, sage, and thyme)

4 Tbls unsalted butter, softened

Olive oil

Kosher salt

Black pepper

Ancho chili powder (optional)

1 cup white wine

**Serves 4**

Preheat oven to 375 degrees

Chop a tablespoon of herbs and mix them with with the butter. Set aside.

Place the chicken on a cutting board, breast side down. Using a good pair of kitchen scissors, cut up each side of the chicken's backbone and through the wishbone. Remove the backbone. Flip the chicken over, making sure the legs are fully splayed open and push down on it to make it lay flat.

Lightly oil a low sided roasting pan or baking tray. Lay the leeks, carrots, garlic cloves and remaining fresh herbs in a layered pile in the center of the pan. Sprinkle with salt and pepper.

Lay the chicken, breast side up over the vegetables, to cover. Loosen the skin covering the chicken and stuff the herbed butter under it, rubbing it around to coat as much of the meat as you can. Smooth out the skin. Drizzle chicken lightly with olive oil and sprinkle to taste with salt, black pepper and ancho chili powder if using.

Pour white wine around the chicken and carefully place the pan in the oven. Roast until meat thermometer registers 160 when inserted between the thigh and breast, about 45 minutes – 1 hour. Baste chicken with pan juices every 15 minutes and if pan goes dry, add more wine or water.

Remove from oven and let stand for 10 minutes before cutting. Serve with delicious vegetables from under the chicken.

VARIATIONS
Use sweet onions, slices of orange and sprigs of lavender under the chicken
Season under the skin with marjoram and butter

Two people from class went home and roasted it over onions, garlic and lemon drizzled with sesame oil. In the butter, they mixed minced fresh ginger, scallions and crushed red pepper and inserted this under the skin

In the winter I like doing it with onions, mushroom, garlic and sundried tomatoes under the chicken and stuffing with fresh basil in the butter under the skin.

# Braised Pork
## with balsamic vinegar & tomatoes

*Even with all the food that comes and goes through the door of the café, I still seem to not have anything in my house to cook for dinner on a Sunday night. I rely endlessly on our local grocery store, two miles away (quite a luxury in a small town on an island 30 minutes from anywhere!). Many a winter evening I will be found wandering the meat aisle wondering what I can buy to make with the can of tomatoes and dried herbs I have in my cupboard. The local market labels a cut of pork as their "Boneless Country Pork Ribs" that I know and love. I find it perfect for braising, my favorite way to prepare anything on a cold winter's day.*

*This easy dish cooks up to a wonderfully flavorful meal and is perfect by the woodstove. Serve it in a bowl or over mashed potatoes or pasta.*

1 tablespoon olive oil

2 pounds boneless country style pork ribs

1 medium onion cut into half-moons

2 red, orange, or yellow bell peppers, seeded and diced

6 cloves garlic, chopped

1 28-ounce can tomatoes (San Marzano, if you can), chopped with juice

¼ cup balsamic vinegar

¼ teaspoon or to taste crushed red pepper flakes

¼ cup fresh basil or 1 Tbls dried basil

½ teaspoon dried marjoram

salt and pepper to taste

**Serves 4–6**

Heat a heavy-bottom skillet (not non-stick) over medium-high heat. Add 1 tablespoon olive oil and then add pork. Brown deeply on both sides of meat. Remove from pan and set aside.

Add onions, peppers and garlic to pan and sauté until soft. Add pork, tomatoes, vinegar, crushed red papper flakes, basil, marjoram and salt and pepper to taste. Simmer covered until pork is very tender (about two hours), turning ocasionally.

Uncover and break meat apart into small pieces. Simmer uncovered until sauce is thickened, about 20 minutes, stirring occasionally. Adjust salt and pepper if needed and serve piping hot.

# Cabbage Soup with Kielbasa

*Winter bliss: Totally spent after a day of sledding, I lay back in the snow and breathe in the day. The sky is blue, the sun is warm on my face and I have a pot of cabbage soup on the stove waiting for us at home.*
*And who says you have to go somewhere warm for the winter?*

1 Tbls oil

1 pound of kielbasa or your favorite smoked sausage, quartered and sliced

1 large yellow onion, chopped

1 medium carrot, diced

1 small head of green cabbage, cored and sliced

1 14 oz can tomato puree

4-6 cups chicken or vegetable stock

1 tsp dried thyme

½ tsp dried oregano

¾ tsp dried basil

Salt and pepper to taste

In a medium soup pot, heat oil over medium high heat and add sausage. Saute until lightly browned. Add onion and carrot and saute until just tender. Stir in cabbage and cook until wilted.

Add 4 cups stock, tomato puree and herbs. Liquid should just cover the cabbage. If you need more or want a soupier consistency add the remaining stock. Bring to boil, reduce heat and simmer partially covered for 45 minutes.

While cooking, season with salt and pepper. Adjust seasoning when soup is done.

**This soup will serve 4 as a main course with a salad and bread**

VARIATION
Omit carrots and tomatoes. Add 2 diced yukon gold potatoes with the stock and change herbs to 1 tsp. sage and ¼ tsp. dried thyme or a few sprigs of fresh thyme.

# Shepherd's Pie

*It has been said on the streets that Lily's is "for girls" but I am proud to say that I regularly serve some of the most "manly" men on the Island. They come in covered in anything from bait juice to plaster dust and I feel a serious obligation to make sure they are well fed to continue with their "manly" day. Shepherd's Pie is a favorite at dinner in the café, but it is also one of my fisherman's favorite meals and we often save a piece for him to have at lunch. Traditionally on the island shepherd's pie is made with ground beef or lamb and corn. This version is very hardy, contains no corn, but has a layer of sautéed vegetables over a spicy layer of ground meat. Topped with a thick layer of mashed potato it is perfect for a winter evening with friends by the fire.*

### Potatoes

3 lbs red potatoes

4 Tbls butter

A bit of milk

Salt to taste

½ cup parmesan cheese

½ tsp paprika

### Vegetables

¼ cup olive oil

1 large onion, chopped

2 medium carrots, peeled and chopped

3 stalks of celery, chopped fine

1 tsp salt

1 ¼ tsp paprika

½ tsp black pepper

1 tsp dried basil

1 bay leaf

Preheat the oven to 375 degrees.

Put the potatoes in a pot and cover with cold water by 2 inches. Bring to a boil and reduce to a simmer. Cook potatoes until fork tender. Drain and mash with butter, a bit of milk and salt and pepper to taste. Add enough milk to get a nice firm but creamy mashed potato. Set aside.

Heat oil in a large skillet. Add vegetables and spices and cook them over low heat until soft and translucent, but not browned, about 15 minutes. Put the cooked vegetables in a bowl.

## Meat

2 ½ pounds ground beef

¼ tsp cayenne pepper or to taste

½ tsp black pepper

½ tsp salt

1 Tbls tomato paste

2 Tbls red wine

1 ½ tsp Worcestershire sauce

1 bay leaf

1 ¼ cups ketchup

**Serves 4-6**

Using the same skillet, put beef, salt and pepper in to cook over medium heat. Using your spoon, break the meat into small pieces. When the meat starts to stick to the bottom of the pan add the tomato paste and wine and cook until almost all the liquid is gone from the skillet. Add the Worcestershire sauce, bay leaf and ketchup. Cook until meat is nicely browned and has a glaze to it, about 20 minutes. Adjust seasoning with salt and pepper.

Lightly grease a high sided baking pan approximately 9"x 13". Spread the meat mixture in the bottom of the pan and then cover evenly with the cooked vegetables. Dollop the mashed potatoes over the vegetables and then spread lightly to cover the pie evenly. Sprinkle with parmesan cheese and paprika.

Bake uncovered in a 375° preheated oven for 15 minutes. Turn temperature down to 325° and continue cooking for another 20 minutes, or until golden and bubbly.

Let rest for 15 minutes until serving.

# Beef Tips in Red Wine Sauce

*This is a different take on a classic recipe. Roasting the onions and mushrooms really give this simple dish a deep layer of flavor.*

2 Tbls olive oil

2 pounds of round steak cut into 1" cubes

2 cups of good tasting red wine

1 cup beef or chicken stock

½ tsp dried thyme

¾ tsp dried marjoram

½ tsp dried oregano

Salt to taste

Fresh ground black pepper

1 pound mushrooms, quartered

1 large yellow onion, peeled, cut into quarters and sliced thinly

3 Tbls olive oil

2 Tbls sherry vinegar

1 Tbls potato starch

1½ tsp cold water

**Serves 4-6**

Heat oven to 400 degrees

Sprinkle beef cubes with salt and pepper. Heat 1 tablespoon olive oil over medium high heat in a 3-4 qt. heavy bottomed pot with a tight fitting lid. Brown beef in batches, adding oil as necessary. Brown well, as the caramelizing will add to the overall flavor of the dish. Place all beef back in pan when finished and add red wine. Bring to a boil and cook for 5 minutes. Add stock, dried herbs and salt to taste. Cover pan and cook in a gentle simmer until meat is very tender, about 2 hours.

Toss mushrooms and onions in 3 tablespoons olive oil and sherry vinegar. Season lightly with salt and pepper. Spread in a single layer on a rimmed baking tray and roast in hot oven, turning frequently, until nicely browned and tender, about 25 minutes. Set aside.

When beef is tender add roasted vegetables and season with salt and freshly ground black pepper.

Mix potato starch and water to form a paste. Stir into beef and cook, stirring, until thickened.

Serve over noodles, rice or mashed potatoes.

# Popcorn

*If you have flipped through this book at all I am sure your eyes went up when you saw a recipe for popcorn. You just don't understand what good popcorn can add to your life. I won my friend Janice's grandkids over with my popcorn. People come to my sewing circle on Mondays for my popcorn. I sneak my popcorn into all the local movie theatres and at Christmas time I sell gift baskets with the three simple fixings to make my popcorn. Try it. It doesn't take but a moment longer than waiting for that butter brushed Styrofoam in the microwave and you will gain friends and influence people. Plus grapeseed oil is good for you.*

2/3 cup of organic yellow popcorn

7 Tbls grapeseed oil

Sea salt to taste

In a 5qt pot heat the oil over high heat.

Add the popcorn and put the lid on with a bit of space for steam to escape.

When the popcorn starts to pop lift the pot (with pot holders) just over the heat and move it around over the heat until you hear the popcorn stop popping.

Pour it into a bowl and season with salt while still warm. Enjoy.

If you like seasoning, try:
Dill and brewers yeast
Chipotle powder and granulated garlic
My favorite is to have some sharp cheddar cheese at room temperature. Eat some cheese and then eat a handful of popcorn. It is the best cheese popcorn you will ever have.

**This recipe makes enough to share.**

# Cornmeal Cake with Honey & Nuts

*Over the years Christmas Eve has turned into a celebration that I really enjoy. Renee makes the wreathes and garland to adorn the house and I get to make a fancy meal. Anyone is invited who has no other obligations and each year I watch acquaintances become friends as we all share our stories while celebrating the season around the candlelit table. I often make this cake and serve it with whipped cream and fresh fruit. A nice ending to a lovely evening.*

■ Gluten Free

1 ½ cups yellow cornmeal

½ cup finely chopped nuts (I use pecans)

2 ½ tsp baking powder

½ tsp salt

1 ¾ sticks unsalted butter at room temperature

½ cup honey

1 tsp pure vanilla extract

3 large egg whites

10 pecan halves

Preheat oven to 350 degrees. Butter a 9" springform pan. Wrap outside of pan with foil to prevent any leakage. Mix cornmeal, chopped nuts, baking powder and salt in a small bowl. Beat butter in a large bowl until light and fluffy. Gradually beat in honey and vanilla. Stir in cornmeal mixture. The batter will be quite stiff. In a separate bowl beat egg whites until soft peaks form. Fold egg whites into cornmeal batter in three additions, gently combining until completely mixed together. Pour batter into pan and space the whole nuts around the outside edge of the cake in an evenly spaced circle.

Bake until cake is golden and tester in center comes out clean. About 35-40 minutes. The sides of the cake will pull away from the pan. Cool cake in pan. Center of cake will fall as it cools. Remove cake from pan and serve at room temperature.

## Whipped Cream

1 cup heavy cream

¼ cup confectioners sugar

½ tsp pure vanilla extract

For whipped cream topping, combine all three ingredients and beat until soft peaks form.

If you make it before dinner, store it in the fridge and if the cream separates just whisk it back together.

**Serves 6-8**

# Apple Streusel Coffee Cake

*A quick and easy cake to make, this is great to have on hand for tea and that unexpected guest.*

## Streusel Topping

½ cup brown rice flour, if available you can substitute ¼ cup chestnut flour for ¼ cup rice flour

¼ cup toasted nuts, chopped

½ tsp cinnamon

¼ tsp nutmeg ( preferably freshly grated)

¼ tsp cardamom

Pinch of sea salt

1 ½ Tbls sunflower oil

1 Tbls pure maple syrup

## Cake

1 ¼ cups brown rice flour

¼ cup tapioca flour

2 ¼ tsp baking powder

¼ tsp sea salt

¼ cup sunflower oil

½ cup brown rice flour

½ cup apple juice

1/3 cup unsweetened soy milk or regular milk

1 ½ tsp pure vanilla extract

2 medium apples, peeled, cored and roughly chopped

Preheat oven to 350 degrees and lightly grease a 9" square baking pan.

Prepare the streusel. Mix together the flour, nuts, spices and salt. With a pastry blender or your fingertips work in oil and syrup to form a moist crumb. Set aside.

Prepare the cake.

Mix the dry ingredients in a large bowl with a whisk to combine. Whisk the wet ingredients in another bowl until well combined. Stir the wet ingredients into the dry and whisk until smooth and thickened. Fold the apples into the batter and pour the batter into the prepared baking pan. Sprinkle the streusel mixture evenly over the top of the cake and bake in preheated oven until cake tests done in the middle with a toothpick, approximately 35-40 minutes.

Allow cake to cool to room temperature.

NOTE: Brown Rice Syrup is found in natural food stores and is sweetener made from brown rice and water.

TIP: Gluten free baked products seem to taste better if allowed to cool completely. Their shelf life is about 2 days.

# Decadent Chocolate Brownie Cake

*In the beginning, when I was diagnosed with being Gluten Intolerant. it was like a bad movie. Sort of on par with putting a newly recovering alcoholic behind the bar on a Friday night. But as time went on and I began to feel so much better from my diet changes, the commitment became quite natural. Of course I have been experimenting like crazy with alternative baked goods that I can have on my counter at home. With the growing awareness of wheat and gluten intolerance in our country I also feel a stronger demand for these items on the counter at the café.*

*It is important to me that my baked goods contain only natural ingredients and that they have no refined sugar. I am excited to include some of these recipes in this book.*

 Gluten Free

❖ Sugar Free

1 ½ cups sweet brown rice flour (brown rice flour may be substituted)

½ cup tapioca flour

1 cup best quality unsweetened cocoa powder

2 teaspoons baking powder

1 teaspoon baking soda

½ teaspoon salt

½ cup sunflower oil (or other light oil, such as almond)

Scant cup brown rice syrup (available at your natural food store)

2 Tbls maple syrup

¾ cup apple juice or cider

¾ cup soy milk or regular milk

1 Tbls vanilla

Preheat oven to 350 degrees.

Lightly grease a 9"x13" pan or two 9" round cake pans. ( I use grapeseed oil spray. Be aware that Canola oil is not on the safe list for gluten intolerance.)

Whisk dry ingredients in a large bowl.

Whisk wet ingredients together completely and add to dry ingredients.

Continue to whisk until you create a smooth batter.

Pour batter into prepared pan and bake 25-30 minutes or until firm to touch and moist crumbs adhere to toothpick inserted in the center of the cake.

Remove from oven and allow to cool on wire rack.

Serve warm or at room temperature.

## Chocolate Sauce

If you would like to sweeten the cake a bit more and make it completely decadent here is a wonderful sauce to pour over the cake when you serve it.

In a medium sauce pan heat together 1 ½ cups pure maple syrup and 2 cups cocoa powder ,sifted. Simmer a few minutes, remove from heat and add 1 teaspoon vanilla.

Makes about 2 cups

## Almond Cream Frosting

This is a last minute addition to the book because I was craving a decadent chocolate layer cake and came up with this concoction.

Place 2 cups of almonds in the bowl of a food processor and process until very fine, almost like powder. This takes a few minutes, so be patient.

With the processor running add ½ cup of brown rice syrup until a paste forms. You can stop here if you want almond paste. I wanted something like frosting so now with the processor running add in a steady stream soy milk, almond milk, half and half, whatever you desire until the paste turns into a thick cream. Voila, almond cream. Let your imagination go wild with the uses of this decadent stuff.

NOTE: I baked the chocolate cake in layers, spread some fruit sweetened raspberry jam on a layer, topped it with almond cream, put the top layer on, spread that with jam and then frosted the cake with the rest of the almond cream. To die for. Renee even swooned over it.

# Spring

It's funny, all winter long I am quite content to sit by the woodstove and nestle in. But as soon as that sun shifts and the smell of the air changes the cat and I are waiting at the back door to set up the screened-in porch, invite friends over, kick back and say hallelujah we made it!!

Now in other parts of the country you would be doing this in April, but for us, it really happens about mid May. The black flies are just waking up and many of our seasonal friends have returned to their summer homes. A real cause for celebration.

# Whole Wheat Apple Date Muffins

1 ¼ cups whole wheat pastry flour

1 ¼ cups unbleached all purpose white flour

½ cup wheat germ

¼ cup packed brown sugar

2 tsp cinnamon

½ tsp nutmeg

¼ tsp mace

2 ½ tsp baking powder

¾ tsp baking soda

½ tsp salt

6 Tbls unsalted butter, melted

1 cup buttermilk

1 egg

1 tsp vanilla

3 Tbls honey

2 cups diced apples

½ cup chopped dates

**Makes 12 muffins**

*Great when you want some whole grain and natural sweetness.*

Preheat oven to 350 degrees. Grease 12 muffin cups or line with paper liners.

Whisk together dry ingredients in large bowl. Whisk together wet ingredients in a medium bowl. Stir the wet ingredients into the dry, just enough to combine. Fold in apples and dates. Fill muffin cups with batter and bake 20 minutes or until cracked on top and toothpick in center comes out clean.

# May Wine

*Life unfolds in mysterious ways. One spring, while wandering around a local garden shop I found an herb called sweet woodruff. The label said it grew well in shaded woodland spots and continued to spread year after year. Sounded perfect for my shaded yard and I planted it. That winter I read in a magazine about the tradition of May wine. You marinate the wine with sweet woodruff which seems to be at its best in mid May. Now I couldn't very well pass up that opportunity. Thus began my yearly tradition of a May wine dinner party. I'll never forget that first year. There was a profusion of white violets in the garden at the restaurant and I had made fat bouquets of them for the table. We ate out on the screened in porch and it happened to be one of my guest's birthday. A wonderful greeting of spring and the anticipation of summer.*

**750 ml bottle of a good Riesling.**
(I always ask for a suggestion at my favorite wine shop)

**Three long sprigs of Sweet Woodruff**

(Woodruff is a perennial herb that is very easy to grow in a shaded part of your yard.)

Open the wine the night before your gathering and stuff the sprigs of Sweet Woodruff in the bottle. Put the cork back in the bottle and let the wine marinate over night.

Serve chilled.

TIP: Pungent soft cheeses go very nicely with the wine.

**Makes 4 to 5 glasses**

# Avoglemeno

*Spring unfolds slowly on the island. Winter tries to fool us with April snow showers and the nights remain cold for some time. But then, all of a sudden it is like the earth just wakes up and we all respond accordingly. Pick-up trucks loaded with traps start barreling to the shore, the peepers start singing in the pond down the road, and the chickens start laying eggs like you wouldn't believe! Last spring at some point, Laurie counted 65 dozen eggs in our refrigerator. I thank the universe daily for the two wonderful men named Peter who supply these fresh ,multi colored, bright yellow, delicious gems to us. We make egg salad, quiche and many people's favorite, this wonderful Greek lemon soup.*

8 cups strong chicken stock

½ cup orzo or rice

8 large eggs yolks, or 6 large eggs

¼ -⅓ cup fresh lemon juice

1 ½ tsp fresh dill, or ½ tsp dried.

More dill to taste

Salt and pepper to taste

**Serves 4 as a main course**

Bring chicken stock to a boil in a medium soup pot. Add orzo or rice and simmer until tender, about 15 minutes.

In a stainless steel bowl, whip eggs and lemon juice together by hand with a whisk until light and frothy.

Very gradually add the egg mixture to the stock, stirring constantly, being very careful not to let the eggs curdle. When all the eggs are in and the soup is smooth and creamy turn off the heat.

Add the dill and let the soup sit for 15 minutes.

# Fresh Lobster Spring Rolls

*A few years ago we were invited to a dinner party at the newly built home of Walter and Linda. It is a lovely three story contemporary house, built overlooking the woods of Mountainville and its surrounding islands. We had cocktails on the outside deck of the third floor. It felt like we were sitting on a ledge in the middle of the forest, which is memorable enough, but then Linda brought out these wonderful spring rolls. Lobster and vegetables wrapped in rice paper with a ginger soy dipping sauce. They were so succulent that I started carrying the rice wrappers at the café and have made them many times since for my own dinner parties. They are always a hit and a wonderful way to use the bounty of lobster that we enjoy in Maine.*

*Any variation of ingredients works here. You don't even have to use lobster. Make them vegetarian and use bean sprouts, or use crab or pork, etc.*

## For the spring rolls

1 head of butter lettuce

1 carrot, cut into 2-inch matchsticks pieces and julienned

1 cucumber, seeds removed and cut into 2-inch matchsticks

20 fresh basil leaves

20 sprigs of cilantro

40 2-inch pieces of fresh chive

1/3 cup coarsely chopped cashews

20 6-inch rice wrappers

¼ cup rice wine vinegar

½ to 1 pound fresh lobster meat cut into ½-inch pieces

Lay out twenty (20) 2" pieces of lettuce and assemble the ingredients in each leaf starting with the veggies, then the herbs and ending with the lobster and nuts.

The tricky part is the rice wrappers. Thanks to Linda's tip, I boil enough water in a large skillet, turn off the heat and add the rice wine vinegar. Then you dip the rice wrappers in the water and allow them to stand for about 15-20 seconds until they are soft. Remove them from the water using tongs and lay out flat on a damp cloth or paper towel.

Place lettuce leaf packet in upper third of the wrapper. Fold in each side and roll.

## For the dipping sauce:

Juice of 1 lime

1 Tbls rice wine vinegar

½ cup chopped cilantro and basil leaves mixed together

1 Tbls minced fresh ginger

2 Tbls soy sauce or tamari

1 cup oil (peanut is traditional, but I use sunflower; try to stay away from olive oil)

**Serves 6**

Whisk lime juice, vinegar, herbs, ginger and tamari together. Whisk in oil in a steady stream until sauce is thickened and completely blended. Adjust seasoning with salt and pepper.

(If you want them spicy, you could add wasabe paste or chili paste to the packet for some punch)

Serve on a platter drizzled with some of the dipping sauce and the rest on the side for individual dipping.

# Gourmet Chicken Fingers

*By late spring the summer people have begun to arrive. Glad to see many of them, we trade winter stories and I watch as they settle down into their island routines. Business begins to pick up and I look forward to weekends filled with summer activities. Music seems to fill the air. Friends from all over gather for a tune at someone's house. Some come to play, others come to listen and I hope to spend the evening dancing. Food and drink is shared along with laughter and memories. The natural talents of people that live on the island never ceases to amaze me. I am truly grateful to be able to partake in the joys of their efforts.*

*I began using rice cakes as a form of gluten free bread crumbs to make these delicious chicken fingers. The crumbs make a nice crunchy coating and seem to be favored by bread and non-bread eaters alike.*
*For an extra special version of this chicken check out the recipe in the variation column.*

3-4 boneless breast of chicken

6 rice cakes

1 Tbls chopped fresh marjoram or 1 tsp dried (oregano may be substituted)

¼ cup freshly grated parmesan cheese

½ ounce dried porcini mushrooms, ground into a powder in a food processor or spice grinder

1 tsp sea salt

½ tsp freshly ground black pepper

Pinch of cayenne pepper

2 eggs

Vegetable oil for pan frying

**Serves 4-6 people as an entrée or 8-10 as an appetizer**

Lay chicken breasts on counter between two pieces of plastic wrap. With the side of hammer or a meat mallot, pound the breasts to a ½-inch thickness. Cut into 1-inch wide strips.

Toast the rice cakes in a toaster or oven until lightly browned. Using a food processor or blender, grind them into a find crumb. Toss the crumbs with the herbs, cheese, mushrooms, salt and peppers. Place half the crumbs on a large plate. In a medium bowl, beat the eggs until frothy. Dip the strips of chicken into the egg, letting the excess drip off. Roll the strips in the seasoned crumbs on the plate, coat lightly, but completely. Lay the coated strips on a tray until you have coated all of them. Add more crumbs to the plate as necessary. Store extra crumbs in an airtight container in the refrigerator up to two weeks.

Heat ½" of oil in a large non stick skillet. Fry the chicken strips in batches until golden brown and cooked through, 2-3 minutes per side. Remove to paper towels to drain. Serve warm. I like to use either homemade or a good quality jarred tomato sauce as a dipping sauce along side the chicken fingers.

## VARIATION

For a really special treat, leave the breasts whole and don't pound them out. Using a sharp knife, make a pocket on the thicker side of each breast. Cut into the breast about ½ inch from one end, slicing to about ¼ inch of the other side. Fill the pocket with fresh mozzarella, thinly sliced ham, sun dried tomatoes and fresh basil leaves. Hold the pocket together, dip the breast into the beaten egg and then into the bread crumb mixture. Refrigerate for 10 minutes to help filling stay in pocket while frying. Turn your oven to 350 degrees. Heat ½ inch of oil over medium high heat in a large non-stick skillet. Cook breasts in oil until golden brown on both sides, about 3 minutes per side. Place on baking tray and finish cooking in oven, about 15 more minutes or until a meat thermometer registers 165 degrees.

TIP: Experiment with stuffing ingredients. Sometimes I marinate the breasts first in oil, wine and herbs for even more flavor. Have fun.

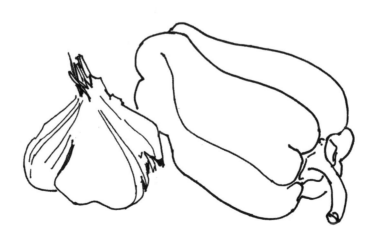

# Lemon Grilled Whole Chicken

*My Uncle Steve is a pure city boy. Raised in New York and living outside Philadelphia he thoroughly enjoys all that a big city has to offer. Sneakers and bug spray are about as foreign to him as wing tips and ties to a fisherman. So is the quiet and the lack of people and he often mentions how dark it gets here at night. We drag him out on the boat and make him hike through the woods to get to the shore. He has learned to arrive after black fly season, but before the crowds hit and is always quite interested in how my life is progressing in such a funny place. In anticipation of his arrival I will often throw a chicken on the grill so I can spend time visiting, not cooking, while he is here.*

1 whole chicken about 3-4 pounds

½ cup fresh lemon juice

Kosher salt

Fresh ground black pepper

Olive oil

Fresh marjoram

**Serves 4**

Rinse chicken and pat dry. Season with salt and pepper. Place chicken in a bowl that is a tight fit. Pour lemon juice and olive oil over chicken and let it sit, breast side down for ½ hour. Turn and let sit another 15 minutes.

Prepare charcoal grill for indirect heat. This means that the fire is to the sides of the meat, not directly underneath. Stuff cavity of chicken with fresh marjoram. (If you don't have that use thyme, or rosemary or even parsley) Grill chicken with cover tightly on grill until a meat thermometer inserted between the breast and thigh registers 160 degrees (about 1 hour to 1 hour and 15 minutes) Remove chicken from heat and let rest for 15 minutes before carving. In the summer I like to serve it at room temperature with simple things like potato salad and grilled vegetables.

# Baked Beans

*Five years ago at Lily's we began a celebration of the season's first batch of maple syrup with our Maple Fest. John and Jen of Carding Brook Farm (who supply me with most of my produce all summer long) bring gallons of their freshly made maple syrup and we have a buffet breakfast on the Saturday of Maple Weekend in Maine. The syrup is delicious and marks the passing of winter and the hopes of spring. John cooks the blueberry pancakes, guest chef's scramble the eggs. There are bacon and scones and oodles of maple syrup. Freed from the stove, I get to chat and laugh with everyone as they come in and really have a good time. My maple baked beans have become quite a hit, too. This recipe makes a big batch, but they freeze well and are great to have around for summer barbecues.*

2 pounds yellow eye beans

1 Tbls salt

2 medium onions, chopped

4 tsp dry mustard

2 tsp ground ginger

½ cup molasses

½ cup maple syrup

½ cup apple cider vinegar

½ pound bacon diced (or if you can get the fatty end of a piece of prosciutto from a good deli the flavor is unbeatable)

**Serves 6**

Place the beans in a big soup pot and cover with cold water by 2 inches. Bring to a boil, add 2 teaspoons of salt and simmer until the beans are just becoming tender, about 2 hours. Drain, discarding cooking water.

Preheat oven to 325 degrees.

Combine the onion, mustard, ginger, molasses, syrup, vinegar and remaining teaspoon of salt in a 6 qt covered casserole dish or bean pot. Add the beans and enough water to cover by half an inch. Poke the bacon or prosciutto into the beans and cover the pot. Bake for 3 hours, stirring them every 45 minutes and making sure there is enough water in the pot to keep the beans soupy at all times. After three hours, uncover the pot and cook an additional 45 minutes to an hour until the sauce thickens and the top is golden brown.

# Sauteed Baby Artichokes & Fingerling Potatoes

*This is a match made in heaven. The grocery store in Ellsworth carries containers of baby artichokes and I scoop up fingerling potatoes as soon as they hit the farm stand. Please feel free to substitute small red or white all purpose potatoes if there are no fingerlings to be found.*

1 ½ pounds fingerling potatoes

1 pound package of baby artichoke hearts

3 Tbls olive oil

4 large cloves of garlic, sliced

1 cup vegetable stock

1 Tbls fresh thyme or 1 tsp dried

Kosher salt

Black pepper

**Serves 4-6 as a side dish**

Rinse potatoes and cut them in half lengthwise. Place in a pot and cover with cold water. Bring to boil, reduce heat and simmer, uncovered, until crisp-tender, about 5 minutes. Drain and dry with paper towels.

Meanwhile, peel leaves from artichokes until you get to the tender yellow ones. Cut the tip and stem from the artichoke and slice them in half. Place them in a bowl of cold water with 1 Tbls lemon juice added to keep them from turning brown while you finish the rest.

Heat oil over medium high heat in a large heavy bottom skillet. Add garlic and cook for 30 seconds. Add artichokes and saute for 2 minutes or until lightly browned. Add the potatoes, thyme and salt and pepper to taste. Stir. Add stock and bring to a boil. Cover, reduce heat to a simmer and cook until vegetables are tender, 15-20 minutes. You want most of the liquid to cook off, but don't let the vegetables burn. Add a tablespoon or more of stock to keep them moist while cooking.

When tender, remove the lid, turn the heat to high and brown vegetables before serving.

NOTE: You can substitute red or Yukon Gold potatoes for the fingerlings.

# Grilled Chicken with Roasted Fiddleheads
## & sweet Vidalia onion

*Fiddleheads are a true spring delicacy in Maine. They are the unfurled tops of a certain type of fern that grows wild in the woods. Don't overcook them or they will get mushy. If you can't get fiddleheads, asparagus would be a nice substitute.*

4 boneless breasts of chicken

2 Tbls olive oil

2 Tbls Balsamic Vinegar

1 Tbls chopped fresh rosemary or 1 tsp dried

1 pound fresh fiddleheads, brown tips trimmed off

2 large Vidalia (or other sweet onion) onions, peeled and cut into 1½-inch chunks

4 Tbls olive oil

Salt and pepper to taste

Balsamic Vinegar and rosemary to finish off roasted vegetables

**Serves 4**

Preheat oven to 425 degrees.

Mix 2 tablespoons oil with 2 tablespoons vinegar and brush on both sides of each chicken breast. Sprinkle evenly with rosemary and season with salt and pepper. Let rest while you get your grill ready.

When grill is hot, grill chicken breasts until firm and just cooked through, about 7 minutes per side.

Meanwhile, bring a pot of salted water to a boil, place fiddleheads in hot water and blanch for 2 minutes. Quickly drain from hot water and run cold water over them to stop the cooking. Place fiddleheads and onions in two separate bowls. Drizzle with remaining olive oil and season with salt and pepper. Toss vegetables to coat with oil and spread each one in a single layer on separate baking trays. Roast in oven, turning occasionally, until tender, but still firm, and dark golden brown. The onions take about 25 minutes, but the fiddleheads will roast in close to 10 minutes so I start the onions first and put the fiddleheads in at the end of the onions' cooking time. Remove from oven and toss together with a splash of balsamic vinegar and a sprinkle of rosemary.

Serve chicken breasts topped with roasted vegetables over rice.

# Braised Halibut with Tomatoes,
## basil & black olives

*I had to include this method of cooking fresh halibut, which we get a lot of in the spring. It is easy to overcook halibut, leaving it dry, but with braising you get great flavor and insured moistness.*

1 ½ pounds fresh halibut, cut into 4 equal servings

2 Tbls olive oil

1 cup stock, white wine or water

14 ounce can diced tomatoes

1 tsp fresh grated lemon peel

¼ cup chopped fresh basil leaves

⅛ cup chopped kalamata or other black olives

Salt and pepper to taste

**Serves 4**

Heat oil in large skillet (not non-stick). Add halibut and sear on both sides, about 1 ½ minutes per side. Add stock, tomatoes, lemon peel, basil, olives and salt and pepper. Bring to a boil, reduce heat, cover fish and simmer until just firm in the center, about 6 minutes. Turn off heat and let rest for 5 minutes. I serve this with rice or potatoes.

# Spaghetti with Wild Chanterelles,
## fresh peas & tarragon

*Chanterelle mushrooms grow wild in dark corners of the forest all over Deer Isle. To insure that I would not wander aimlessly and ingest something that would kill me, my Aunt took me on a wonderful search through the woods. We found enough so that I could identify them, but not enough to really cook with. A few years later Renee and I were walking through a forest in Sunshine and stumbled upon a whole patch of the beautiful things. We gathered them in our shirts, invited my Aunt and Uncle over for supper and gorged ourselves. It wasn't until the "mushroom lady" Pam Pace wandered into the café last year with a whole basket of them, hoping to exchange them for some sweets, that I could actually be creative. I gladly emptied the basket and filled it with brownies, cakes and cookies and began planning that evening's menu. It was late spring, the tarragon outside the door looked like a bush and fresh peas were on the farm stand. The combination over pasta is a wonderful seasonal treat.*

¼ cup olive oil

8 ounces chanterelle mushrooms, sliced thickly

½ cup chopped scallions

1 cup shelled fresh peas

½ cup white wine

2 Tbs fresh tarragon

½ cup heavy cream

Salt and pepper to taste

1 pound spaghetti, cooked al dente

Heat oil over medium heat in a large heavy-bottomed skillet. Add mushrooms and scallions, sauté until just getting soft. Add peas and salt to taste, cook for just 1 minute. Add wine, turn heat to high and reduce liquid by half. Add cream, tarragon and freshly ground black pepper. Simmer until cream begins to thicken, about 3 minutes. Stir in pasta; toss in the sauce over heat until coated, about 3 minutes.

NOTE: This recipe can be made with Baby Portabella or any firm mushroom.

**Serves 4**

# Baked Ziti with Roasted Eggplant
## & fresh mozzarella cheese

*Neither my Mother nor my Aunt boast diamond rings, diamond anything for that matter. Quite frankly I had resolved that a beautiful diamond was out of my reach. But, as it often does, an opportunity arose.*

*I had decided that I was ready for a newer model of my Passat Stationwagon. Robin, a brilliant jeweler, wanted to buy my old one, but immediate finances prevented her from making that happen. One day in passing I shyly mentioned that maybe we could trade, a diamond ring for the car. Her eyes lit up and the rest is history. She scoured her sources for the perfect old European diamond and seemed to know what I wanted the ring to look like without much conversation. On the eve of the exchange, Robin, her husband, their two year old son and a friend came for dinner. The two moments I remember most are my beautiful diamond ring shimmering in the candle light and her two year old son eating a whole plate of this delicious baked ziti.*

3 small Italian eggplants

6 Tbls olive oil

1 Tbls salt

2 large cloves of garlic, peeled and sliced

2 (28-ounce) cans San Marzano tomatoes

½ tsp crushed red pepper flakes, or more to taste

1 ½ cups fresh basil leaves, ripped

1 tsp salt

1 pound ziti pasta

4 ounce ball fresh mozzarella cheese cut into ¼-inch cubes

½ pound fresh ricotta cheese (if you are lucky enough to be able to get it) or 1 pound packaged whole milk ricotta cheese

Parmesan cheese

**Serves 4-6**

Preheat oven to 400 degrees. Peel eggplant or leave strips of skin on, your choice. Cut into 1-inch cubes. Spread 3 tablespoons oil on a sheet tray, roll eggplant around in oil to coat. Arrange in a single layer and roast until crispy and dark golden brown, turning once in oven, about 25 minutes.

Bring 6 quarts of water and 1 tablespoon salt to boil in a large pot. Add ziti and cook until al dente. Follow package directions, usually between 7-10 minutes depending on the pasta. Drain and return to cooking pot.

In a large skillet heat the remaining 3 tablespoons of oil, add the garlic slices and cook until just starting to turn golden. With your hands, crush the tomatoes lightly and add to the pan with the garlic and oil. Season with 1 teaspoon of salt and the crushed red pepper flakes. Bring to a boil, reduce heat and simmer for 12 minutes, stirring occasionally. Stir in the fresh basil and adjust salt.

Stir ¾ of the sauce into the cooked pasta. Add eggplant and mozzarella. Pour pasta into a greased lasagna pan, approximately 13" x 11". Push heaping teaspoons of ricotta cheese into pasta, evenly distributing the cheese. Pour remaining sauce over pasta and top with sprinkling of parmesan cheese.

Bake in preheated oven until bubbling and lightly browned, 20-30 minutes.

# Cajun Halibut with Lime Garlic Olive Oil

*One afternoon I was cleaning lettuce in the back kitchen of the café. I heard someone under the window and looked to find a handsome young fisherman asking if I wanted to buy a fish. Who could turn down an offer like that? The fish was a beautiful fresh Halibut, just caught that day. Fortunately for me, I get that offer a lot during Halibut season. The combination of cajun spice and roasting the filets in oil really seems to do this meaty white fish justice.*

## Cajun Seasoning
Mix together:
2 ½ Tbls paprika, 2 Tbls salt, 2Tbls granulated garlic, 1 Tbls black pepper, 1 Tbls cayenne, 1 Tbls dried oregano, 1 Tbls dried thyme. Store extra in an airtight container for another day.

(4) 6-8 ounce fresh halibut filets

1 cup olive oil

Grated peel from one lime

⅓ cup fresh lime juice

4 cloves garlic, chopped

**Serves 4**

Preheat oven to 425 degrees

Coat the top of each filet with cajun seasoning and allow to stand at room temperature for 20 minutes, or keep refrigerated until ready to cook.

Whisk together the oil, lime and garlic

Place the fish filets in a 9" glass baking dish. The fish should be crowded, but not overlapping.

Pour the oil mixture over the fish and bake for 10-12 minutes in hot oven. Do not overcook or the fish will be dry. It is done when the center is just firm but still moist.

# Chocolate Cheesecake Bars
## with raspberry jam

*The earliest memory I have of just messing around with food in a kitchen without any recipe is as a child summering in Sunshine. Cindy Dill and I collected buckets of wild blueberries growing around our camps and made cookies without any idea what we were doing. They came out okay and to this day I love to mess around with food in the kitchen and see what I come up with. Some of it isn't very good, but sometimes I make something memorable, like these bars.*

### Bottom Layer

2 cups unbleached all purpose flour

½ cup sugar

16 Tbls unsalted butter, at room temperature

½ cup chocolate chips

2 cups seedless raspberry jam

### Cheesecake filling

1 pound cream cheese, at room temperature

½ cup sugar

2 eggs

2 tsp pure vanilla extract

6 ounces chocolate chips, melted

½ pint fresh raspberries
Chocolate shavings or miniature chocolate chips

### Makes 24 2-inch squares

Preheat oven to 350 degrees.

Place the flour, sugar and chocolate chips in the bowl of a food processor. Process until combined and the chips are broken up. Add butter and process until dough is moist and just beginning to stick together.

Press dough evenly into a greased 9" x13" baking pan.

Bake for 15 – 20 minutes, until crust is set and lightly browned. Remove from oven and let cool for 10 minutes. Spread jam evenly over bottom layer to cover. (an offset spatula works the best)

Cream together the cream cheese and sugar until fluffy. Add the eggs and vanilla and beat until smooth. Beat in the melted chocolate until well blended. Dollop the cheesecake filling onto the jam layer and carefully spread to cover jam completely. Bake in oven until cheesecake filling is slightly cracked around the edges, but just barely set in the center. Remove from oven and allow to cool completely.

Cut into squares and decorate with fresh raspberries and chocolate shavings.

VARIATION: STRAWBERRY LIME BARS
Omit the chocolate chips in the bottom layer and add grated zest of 1 lime.
Spread crust with strawberry jam.
Omit the chocolate chips and vanilla in the cheesecake filling and add ½ cup fresh lime juice. Top with fresh strawberries and shavings of coconut.

# Chocolate Almond Butter Cookies

*I have a wicked soft spot for rainy spring Saturdays at home. My sweat pants are on, there are cookies in the oven and my sewing machine is waiting. If I feel really decadent I don't even sew. I just lie on the couch and watch movies, eating cookies and popcorn with the cat curled up under my arm.*

 Gluten Free

❖　Sugar Free

1 ¼ cups brown rice flour

½ cup unsweetened cocoa powder

¼ cup sweet brown rice flour

2 tsps baking powder

¼ tsp sea salt

½ cup almond butter

½ cup sunflower or almond oil

½ cup brown rice syrup

1 tsp pure vanilla extract

**Makes approximately 24 cookies**

Preheat oven to 350 degrees.

Line two baking sheets with parchment paper.

Whisk flours, cocoa, baking powder and salt in a large bowl. Whisk almond butter, oil, rice syrup and vanilla until smooth and combined in a medium bowl. Stir wet ingredients into dry and form a smooth dough. Shape dough into 1 ½ inch balls and place 2 inches apart on prepared trays. Flatten with the tines of a fork as in peanut butter cookies.

Bake 12 – 15 minutes until cookies are just firm to the touch.

Cool completely for the best flavor.

VARIATIONS

Use peanut butter instead of almond butter.

Delete the cocoa and add ½ cup potato starch for a chocolate free cookie.

# Thumbprint Cookies

*With the prodding of Renee to take Nancy Knowlton's beginners quilting class 7 years ago I discovered my true life's passion (other than food and gardening). She had two rules," have fun and no swearing". Determined to prove to my friends that I could make it for 3 hours at a time without saying one four letter word, I set to making my first quilt. Of course I am in love with the fabrics and the colors and the piecing and the stitching, but what I like the most is gathering with very special friends and spending time together laughing, talking and quilting. I introduced these cookies a few years back at a quilting lunch at my home with my friends from Sewing By the Sea and they were a huge hit.*

■ Gluten Free

❖ Sugar Free

1 cup nuts (I often use pecans) toasted and finely chopped

1 ½ cups brown rice flour

½ cup potato starch

½ tsp baking powder

½ tsp cinnamon

¼ tsp sea salt

½ cup sunflower oil

½ cup brown rice syrup

1 tsp pure vanilla extract

½ cup fruit sweetened jam

**Makes approximately 24 cookies**

Preheat the oven to 350 degrees. Line two baking sheets with parchment paper.

Mix dry ingredients in a large bowl. Whisk the oil, syrup and vanilla in a separate bowl until well combined. Stir the wet ingredients into the dry and form into a smooth dough.

Roll into 1 ½ inch balls and place on baking sheets. Make an indentation in each cookie by pressing the center in with your thumb. Fill indentations with jam.

Bake cookies until golden and just firm, about 12-15 minutes. Allow to cool completely.

# Pecan Squares

*Nina went sugar free a few years ago and we are often exchanging recipes and new ideas. She turned me on to a wonderful cookbook called "Sweet and Natural" by Meredith McCarty and brought in a recipe for Cinnamon cookies using almond meal. Being me, I kept fooling with the recipe until it turned into these pecan squares. Honestly, I don't think anyone would know they are made without refined sugar.*

■ Gluten Free

❖ Sugar Free

2 cups pecans, finely chopped

⅓ cup sunflower oil

½ cup brown rice syrup

⅛ tsp sea salt

¼ tsp baking soda

I tsp cinnamon

Preheat oven to 325 degrees and line a 9" square baking pan with parchment paper.

Place the oil, syrup, salt, soda and cinnamon in a bowl and whisk until well combined. Stir in the pecans and coat well. Spread nut mixture into pan and bake until bubbling in the middle, about 20 –25 minutes.

Let cool completely and cut into I-inch squares.

**Makes 70-80 squares**

# Lemon Meringue Pie

*Someone dying is never easy. Sometimes it seems that there has been more than our fair share of losses on the island. I have been honored at Lily's Café to have people seek comfort either in food or conversation during the hard time of change that loss seems to bring to our lives. I have also had many last requests from people for their favorite thing before they go. I don't make one lemon meringue pie without thinking of Dick Billings, the founder of Billings Diesel and Marine.*

### Crust

2 cups unbleached all purpose flour

1 Tbls sugar

1 tsp salt

14 Tbls chilled unsalted butter

4 Tbls cold water

### Filling

1 ½ cups water

1 cup sugar

½ cup fresh lemon juice

6 large egg yolks

5 Tbls cornstarch

2 Tbls grated lemon peel

¼ tsp salt

2 Tbls unsalted butter

Preheat oven to 350 degrees.

Place flour, sugar and salt in the bowl of a food processor. Pulse to combine. Add butter in small pieces and process until well distributed and the flour looks like coarse meal. With the machine running, add the water in a steady stream and process until dough begins to pull together. Gently gather into a ball, flatten slightly, wrap in plastic wrap and refrigerate for 30 minutes.

Roll dough out on a lightly floured surface to an 11" circle. Line a 9" or 10" pie plate with crust, fold edges and crimp decoratively. Line crust with aluminum foil and weigh foil down with beans, rice or pie crust weights. Bake in preheated oven for 10 minutes, remove foil and weights and continue to bake until crust is golden brown, about another 10 minutes. Remove from oven, but leave oven on and allow crust to cool completely.

Whisk first 7 ingredients in heavy medium saucepan to blend. Using a whisk, stir over medium heat until filling thickens and just begins to boil, 15-20 minutes. Remove from heat, stir in butter and pour into cooled crust.

### Meringue

7 large egg whites (that is how I get it so high)

½ tsp cream of tartar

1 ⅔ cups powdered sugar

Using an electric mixer, beat egg whites until foamy. Beat in cream of tartar and 1 tablespoon of sugar, beating until soft peaks form. Add remaining sugar gradually and continue beating until stiff, glossy peaks form, about 8 minutes at medium speed.

Mound meringue on top of warm filling, spreading evenly all the way to outside edges. Make sure you cover the filling completely to the crust to seal the meringue and keep it from shrinking.

Reduce oven temperature to 300 degrees and bake pie until meringue is golden brown and set when shaken slightly, about 30 minutes. Cool completely before cutting.

TIP: To keep meringue pies from weeping store uncovered in the refrigerator.

VARIATION

For rhubarb meringue pie use 4 cups chopped rhubarb, 1 cup sugar, 3 tablespoons cornstarch, 1/8 teaspoon salt, 2 tablespoons unsalted butter. Combine all filling ingredients in a medium saucepan. Bring to boil, stirring constantly. Reduce heat to a simmer and cook 5 minutes or until mixture is thickened. Stir in butter, pour into pie shell and proceed as in lemon meringue pie.

# Rhubarb Custard Pie

*This pie always gets rave reviews. Please use a 10" pie plate or you will have a mess in your oven.*

## Crust

1 ½ cups unbleached all purpose flour

2 Tbls brown sugar

1 tsp cinnamon

9 Tbls chilled unsalted butter

2 Tbls ice water

## Filling

5 cups diced rhubarb (fresh is best)

1 ½ cups sugar

2 large eggs

1 cup sour cream

3 Tbls small tapioca pearls

Pinch of salt

1 tsp pure vanilla extract

## Makes 8 servings

Place flour, sugar and cinnamon in the bowl of a food processor, pulse to combine. Cut butter into small pieces and add to the processor. Process until mixture resembles coarse crumbs. With machine running, add water in a steady stream. Process until dough begins to come together. Remove dough from processor and shape into a disk. Wrap in plastic wrap and chill for 30 minutes. Roll crust out on lightly floured surface to a 12" circle. Line 10" pie plate, trim to 1-inch overhang all the way around. Tuck extra under and crimp edges to form a high decorative crust.

Preheat oven to 400 degrees.

Toss the rhubarb and sugar together in a large bowl. Whisk the eggs, sour cream, tapioca, salt and vanilla extract in a separate bowl and add to the rhubarb mixture, stirring until mixed well. Fill crust lined pie pan and bake in 400 degree oven for 15 minutes.

Meanwhile, make the topping.

## Topping

½ cup packed brown sugar

1 tsp cinnamon

⅓ cup unbleached all purpose flour

½ cup rolled oats

4 Tbls unsalted butter, softened

Mix all ingredients except butter in a small bowl. Using your fingertips or a fork, blend in the butter until a moist crumbly topping appears. After baking pie for 15 minutes, turn the oven to 350, sprinkle the topping evenly over the pie and continue baking until golden brown and the fruit is bubbling, about 50 minutes.

Let pie cool for 1 hour before cutting for the best presentation.

# Summer

Renee has had me out in our boat hauling lobster traps for almost nine years now. We each have five traps and because of Renee's experience as the daughter of a fisherman, we actually catch enough to eat all summer long. Our summer guests love it when she takes them to haul, but I love it most when it is just the two of us. There is nothing like the feeling I get each time in the boat when she rounds the corner at Billings and heads out into the bay. Since I am the "stern man" it is my job to clean the trap of creatures other than lobster and put in new bait. I love dawdling with the sea cucumbers, hermit crabs, starfish and other treasures that come up in the trap and I am often yelled at for wanting to throw back a big lobster, arguing that if it has lived long enough to be that big, we shouldn't eat it.

# Sensational Scones

*Almost every local person's yard boasts laundry hanging on a line. While many a summer artist spends time painting the shirts and sheets blowing in the breeze, I have created the scene in my own yard. When I know that it will be a good day, I put laundry in the washer the night before so that I can hang it out on the line before I go off to work the next morning. It is quiet in my backyard except for the sound of fishing boats leaving the harbor and the birds eating breakfast at the feeder. I often feel more settled when I get to work after hanging laundry and my scones always seem to come out their best.*

2 cups unbleached all purpose flour

½ cup whole wheat pastry flour

½ cup rolled or quick cooking oats

2 tsp baking powder

½ tsp baking soda

¼ tsp salt

1 Tbls sugar

8 Tbls unsalted butter, cut into small pieces

2 eggs

½ - ¾ cup buttermilk at room temperature

2 Tbls maple syrup

1 ½ tsp pure vanilla extract

Preheat oven to 400 degrees.

Whisk flours, oats, baking powder, soda, sugar and salt together in a large bowl. Cut butter in using a pastry blender or your fingertips until pea size and well distributed. In another bowl, using a fork lightly beat together the eggs, buttermilk, maple syrup and vanilla. Pour into the dry mixture and using the fork mix together until you have a shaggy dough. This should only take several turns with the fork. The real trick to good scones is really not over mixing the dough. Gather the dough together and knead gently several times to make it hold together. Gently pat into a 1-inch thick circle. Cut scones with a biscuit cutter and place on an ungreased baking tray.

## Topping

2 Tbls sugar

1 Tbls maple syrup

1 tsp water

Rolled oats

Prepare the topping by whisking the sugar, syrup and water together. Brush each scone with the topping and top with a pinch of rolled oats. Bake in preheated oven 15-20 minutes or until golden and toothpick in the center comes out clean.

**Makes 7-12 scones**

# Raspberry Corn Muffins

*Moist corn muffins dotted with jewels of berries nestled in a basket lined with an aged linen cloth. Ironstone china, fresh flowers and Frank crooning on the radio. I found a wonderful apron from the 40's at a church sale to complete the scene. The morning has brought sun and it is warm enough to sit on the screened-in porch. Friends will be arriving shortly. I love to play house on the weekends.*

1 cup cornmeal

1 cup unbleached all purpose flour

⅓ cup sugar

2 ½ tsp baking powder

¼ tsp salt

1 cup whole milk

6 Tbls unsalted butter, melted

1 egg

2 tsp grated lemon peel

½ pint fresh raspberries or 1 ½ cups frozen

Preheat oven to 375 degrees. Generously butter 12 muffin cups.

In a bowl whisk together the cornmeal, flour, sugar, baking powder and salt.

In another bowl whisk together the milk, butter, egg and lemon peel.

Stir the wet ingredients into the dry and gently stir to combine. Don't overmix.

Fold the berries into the batter and spoon it into the buttered cups.

Bake for 20-25 minutes or until toothpick inserted into center comes out with a few moist crumbs attached.

Allow to cool for 10 minutes before removing from pan.

**This makes 12 small muffins**

NOTE: If you want big muffins, double the recipe and fill the cups to the top. You will get 14.

# Jelly Filled Doughnut Muffins

*Remember jelly doughnuts when you were a kid? Glazed in sugar and oozing with raspberry jelly. My father would come home from the bakery with that white bag in his hand, grease rings on the bottom from the little gems inside. These muffins are a variation of that theme, a bit simpler to make, less greasy but very rewarding.*

2/3 cup unsalted butter, melted and cooled

1 ½ cups milk

2 large eggs

1 ½ tsp pure vanilla extract

3 ½ cups unbleached all purpose flour

½ cup sugar

5 tsp baking powder

1 tsp salt

Raspberry jam

8 Tbls unsalted butter, melted

Granulated sugar

Preheat oven to 375 degrees. Generously butter 12 muffin cups.

Whisk the cooled butter, milk ,eggs and vanilla together in a large bowl. In a medium bowl whisk together the flour, sugar, baking powder and salt to blend. Add the dry ingredients to the wet, stirring just to combine. The batter should still be lumpy. Spoon half the batter into the 12 muffin cups. Place a heaping teaspoon of jam in the center of each cup and top with remaining batter, smoothing to cover the jam.

Bake in preheated oven for 15-20 minutes, or until they are golden brown and firm to the touch.

Allow to cool for 10 minutes. Remove muffins from tin and dip tops in melted butter and roll in granulated sugar.

**Makes 12 muffins**

# Fresh Corn Soup with Basil
## & roasted red pepper

*A few summers ago my Aunt was babysitting her neighbor's garden up the road from her own bountiful glory. She kept telling me that this woman's corn was almost ready and she was to harvest it and not to let it go to waste. So, we would eat it. It was late summer, because I remember the lower angle of the orange sunlight coming in her dining room window when she appeared from the kitchen with a platter of corn on the cob. I had never had corn like this in my life. They were these plump, juicy, long, creamy white ears cooked to perfection and so sweet they didn't need butter or salt. I often swoon over the memory of that corn and have never really had anything like it since.*

*This soup is pure summer in a bowl and relies on just a few fresh ingredients. At the restaurant we make this soup only when the corn is in season. Not that it stops Nichole from asking for it all winter long.*

1 Tbls olive oil

1 small onion chopped

1 large clove of garlic, chopped

4 cups of corn kernels scrapped from the cob, about 6 large ears. (Or if you want this in the winter, use a good frozen corn)

5 cups chicken or vegetable stock

Pinch of cayenne pepper, chipotle powder or smoked hot paprika

1 red pepper, roasted, peeled and diced or 2 quality roasted red peppers from a jar, diced

½ cup fresh basil leaves, chopped.

Salt to taste

Heat the oil over a low flame in a medium soup pot. Add the onions and garlic and cook, covered, until golden. Approximately 10 minutes.

Add corn, stock, roasted red pepper and the cayenne pepper to the pot and bring to a boil. Simmer, partially covered for 25 minutes. Add basil. Taste for salt. Let stand 15 minutes.

You can serve this just like this. For a thicker soup, remove half the corn from the broth, puree it and return it to the pot. This makes the soup creamy and thick.

**Serves 4**

# Soup with Cauliflower
## & spinach linguine

*Once in a while a rainy summer Saturday is a blessing. Honestly, summer is but a moment here. So much gets packed into 3 short months that a day with valid reason to slow down is welcomed. On such an occasion I was thumbing through magazines on the porch and saw an ad for Italy featuring a bowl of clear broth with nuggets of cauliflower swirled by noodles and floating islands of olive oil. Pure comfort food on a rainy day. I had to eat it!!*

*I had cauliflower on hand. So I unfolded myself from my cat on the couch, gathered my ingredients and began to create what I had a vision of.*

*I make this soup all the time now. It is quick and delicious and even if you don't think you like cauliflower, it really works.*

8 cups homemade stock (normally I don't request it, but this soup relies heavily on the quality of the broth.)

Small head of cauliflower, about 2 pounds

½ pound of spinach linguine or other favorite pasta

¼ cup chopped fresh parsley

¼ cup extra virgin olive oil

Sea salt to taste

Freshly grated parmesan cheese

Freshly ground black pepper

**Serves 4**

Place stock in a medium soup pot. Season with salt and bring to a boil.

Meanwhile, remove core from cauliflower and cut into 1" florets. When stock comes to a boil add cauliflower and simmer with the cover on until tender, 5-8 minutes.

Add linguine and cook soup uncovered until pasta is al dente.

Add parsley and turn off heat. Drizzle soup with olive oil and season with salt and pepper.

Serve with freshly grated parmesan cheese.

# Cold Carrot & Cucumber Soup

*This soup reflects a moment in my life before I started owning a restaurant. My friend Susan and I got a 2 week stint cooking for a family in a 15,000 square foot house who wanted to go on vacation but didn't want to travel. How cool is that? We prepared lunch and dinner for them every night for 14 days with a few cocktail and dinner parties thrown into the mix. They were quality conscious, but open to just about anything. It was summer and they were having 8 people to dinner. The creative energy between Susan and I was extraordinary. A few glasses of wine and some good music and we could come up with just about anything.*

*This soup was a last minute decision and has become part of my regular repertoire. It always brings wonderful memories back of us not really knowing what we were doing, but going with our gut and succeeding. We never spilled anything on their Persian carpet in the dining room and we never told anyone that they had plastic lawn furniture in their living room.*

4 cups quality chicken or vegetable stock

1 pound carrots, peeled and cut into small pieces

1 small yellow onion, roughly chopped

Salt to taste

2 medium cucumbers, peeled, seeded and chopped

½ cup sour cream

1-2 Tbls chopped fresh dill

Freshly ground black pepper

Place the stock, carrots, onion and a bit of salt in a medium soup pot. Bring to boil, reduce to a simmer and cook until carrots and onion are tender. Remove from heat and allow to cool to room temperature

When cool, add cucumbers and dill and puree. Whisk in sour cream. Season with salt and pepper to taste.

Chill.

**Serves 4 –6 as first course**

# Leek & Potato Soup with Loads of Fresh Basil

*As I drive by each Maine house that has a barn I know that there is a secret stash of something in each one. Last summer I discovered what one barn was hiding and I couldn't have fantasized about something any better. Well maybe, but this was pretty good. Neighbors of friends had a bumper crop of leeks which they harvested in fall and wintered over in their barn. By summer they were starting to go by and new ones would be coming so they asked if I wanted some. Of course!! I wanted to cook something that would allow me to eat as many leeks as possible in one sitting. I love traditional leek and potato soup, but it being summer, I wanted something a bit lighter. Loads of leeks, lots of fresh basil and I finished it off with soy milk instead of heavy cream, but that is up to you.*

2 Tbls sunflower oil or other light oil

5 cups of sliced leeks, white and light green parts only

1½ pounds red potatoes, sliced thinly

4 cups of chicken or vegetable stock

Salt and pepper to taste

1 cup fresh basil leaves, julienned

1½ cups soy milk or cream

Heat oil in 4-6 qt pot over medium heat. Add leeks and cook covered until tender, stirring occasionally, about 10-15 minutes. Stir in potatoes and cook for 2 minutes. Add stock and salt. The amount of salt will depend on how salty your stock is and your taste preference. (I prefer Kosher in this recipe)

Bring soup to boil and reduce to a gentle simmer. Simmer uncovered until potatoes are very tender. Add basil.

Puree soup in blender. Return to pot and stir in soy milk or cream and adjust salt to taste. Season with freshly ground black pepper and serve.

Can be chilled and served cold also.

TIP: Please, if you are going to use soy milk, which can be interchanged with milk in any recipe, make sure it is a good quality brand like Pacific or Westbrae and check to see that it is unsweetened. The list of ingredients should be: water and soybeans.

TIP: I slice the leeks in half lengthwise and then slice them about ¼-inch thick. Put them in a colander and rinse under cold water to remove any sand or grit.

**Serves 4 as main meal with a salad or 8 as a first course**

# End of Summer Soup

*By Labor Day every working person on this island is exhausted no matter who they are.*

*Busting butt to make the bulk of our earnings in three short months, we are also determined to cram as much social activity into our lives as possible. Since Labor Day is defined in my Webster dictionary as "a day set aside for special recognition of the working man" the café is traditionally closed.*

*At home waiting for me is a bounty of garden vegetables that I haven't had the chance to enjoy.*

*Time to make a pot of soup and invite friends to share (and do the dishes).*

*The ingredients used in this soup vary, depending on what I have a lot of at home. Please use this as a guide and add whatever else you have or take away what you don't have. Usually people are bringing other dishes when I serve this so I don't add meat. If you have any leftover cooked meat it could be added with the corn and spinach.*

1 Tbls olive oil

2 pounds mushrooms, sliced

¼ cup cream sherry

2 Tbls olive or grapeseed oil

4 cups leeks, white and pale green parts only, cut lengthwise and sliced thinly

Bunch of baby carrots, chopped

8 cups of chicken or vegetable stock

Corn, scraped from the leftover cobs in the fridge, about 2 cups

6 cups baby spinach, chopped

3 cloves garlic, minced

1 Tbls fresh rosemary

**Hearty bowl of soup for 6**

In a roomy soup pot heat 1 Tbls olive oil over medium heat and add mushrooms. Saute until water evaporates and mushrooms turn a golden brown.

Add sherry and reduce to a shiny coating on the mushrooms. Add 2 Tbls olive or grapeseed oil to the pot.

Stir in the leeks and cook covered until the leeks are tender, about 10 minutes. Add carrots and garlic and saute for 5 minutes.

Add stock and bring to a boil. Simmer soup for 20 minutes. Add corn, spinach and rosemary.

Continue to simmer for another 15 minutes. Salt and pepper to taste.

# Clam Chowder

*As a child vacationing on Deer Isle, at least one low tide was spent in the mud flats with Mrs. Dill. Her daughter Cindy and I would don our rubber boots and she would carry the clam hoes and rollers. All set to help, I would begin by poking and prodding the mud where the clams were spitting at me through holes in the sand. But really, I was much more worried about loosing my boots in the mud. By the time we had to go I was usually sitting by a tidal pool watching all creatures of the small community go about their business of survival.*

*As an adult living on Deer Isle I often catch glimpses of the guys out on the clam flats at low tide, bent over and moving sand for hours at a time. To make a living, they clam every day, filling three bushels or more of clams a tide and doing double tides on the days of a full moon. Some fill their canoes with their gear and paddle out to their secret places. Others walk a far piece to get to the low water marks. All of them have encountered people from away screaming at them to get off their land. Cold rain, piping hot sun, frozen flats and the fluctuating prices all keep the days challenging. I never make a pot of clam chowder without being grateful for their hard work.*

¼ cup unsalted butter

1 medium yellow onion, chopped

2 cloves of garlic, minced

¼ cup unbleached all purpose flour

8 cups clam juice or 4 cups clam juice and 4 cups water

2 cups diced potatoes

2 stalks celery, chopped

1 tsp dried thyme

1 cup heavy cream or half and half

1 pound shucked raw clams

Dash hot sauce

**Serves 4-6**

Melt butter over low heat in a heavy bottomed soup pot. Add onion and garlic and cook, covered, until golden, 10-15 minutes. Whisk in flour and stir for two minutes until flour cooks. Gradually add the clam juice, whisking to remove any lumps. Add the potatoes, celery, and thyme and bring to a boil. Reduce heat to low and simmer until potatoes are tender, about 20 minutes. Stir in cream and clams and cook until heated through. Do not allow soup to boil. Finish off with a dash of hot sauce.

# Haricots Verts Salad

*My earliest memory of Haystack Mountain School of Crafts, located in Sunshine on Deer Isle, is of watching a man teach glass blowing on a drizzly day in the early 1970's. Later that night, while my parents' listened to a duet of guitar and flute music, I found my way into the kitchen, where a teenage Cindy Billings gave me a brownie. At eight years old I was completely overwhelmed by this magical place and feel that way to this day. People attribute much of the local artist population to the influence Haystack has had on the island. I attribute the idea for this wonderful green bean salad to a dinner I enjoyed before the yearly scholarship benefit auction.*

1 pound of haricots verts green beans (these are the really thin ones)

4 Tbls olive oil

1 large red onion, peeled and sliced into thin rings

2 Tbls vinegar, red wine, sherry, etc.

½ cup Kalamata olives, pitted and sliced

½ cup fresh basil leaves, julienned

1 pint cherry tomatoes, cut in half

Salt and freshly ground pepper to taste

4 ounces of crumbled cheese, feta, bleu, goat etc.

Bring a pot of salted water to a boil. Add beans and blanch until crisp tender, 2-4 minutes. Drain and rinse in cold water to stop them from cooking further.

In a large skillet, heat oil over medium heat. Add onion rings and saute until just getting soft, 4-5 minutes.

Toss in cooled beans, saute a few minutes more and add vinegar. Toss and remove from heat.

Stir in olives, basil, tomatoes and salt and pepper.

Serve warm or at room temperature with a crumble of soft cheese, like feta, goat or bleu.

# Fresh Corn Salsa with Ginger

*Yard Sales are a Saturday morning ritual in the summer. With the course plotted Friday night, we head out around 7am with tote bag in hand, ready to fight the crowds and find our treasures. What a lot of you don't understand is that it is so much more than other people's junk. Early summer mornings here are quietly glorious. We drive all over the Peninsula finding hidden roads and secret short cuts. We have made friends that we only see at yard sales, often catching up while waiting to be let in to a barn or an old house. A lot of the things in my home have come from other people's lives and I often wonder what life a dish or a chair has had prior to its life with me. Snacks are a must while sale hunting. Many people know me because I always have a bag of chips in my hand. This salsa is a wonderful accompaniment.*

1 14-oz. can diced tomatoes (Muir Glen Fire Roasted are the best)

Corn kernels scraped from two cobs (about ¾ cup)

¼ cup black olives, chopped

¼ cup diced sweet onion

1 clove of garlic, chopped

½ tsp or to taste, ground ancho chili

2 tsps grated or minced fresh ginger

Handful of fresh cilantro, chopped

1 Tbls brown rice vinegar

2 Tbls olive oil

Salt and pepper to taste

Dash of Tabasco (optional)

Place all ingredients in a bowl and toss to combine. Adjust seasoning with salt.

For best flavor, let stand for an hour before eating. Enjoy with your favorite chips or use on grilled meats or fish as a wonderful accompaniment.

**Makes approx. 2 ½ cups**

# Potato Salad with Blueberrries

*Don't make that face until you have tried it!!*

1 ½ pounds red potatoes, peeled and cut into 1 inch cubes

½ cup yogurt (Greek yogurt if you have it)

⅓ cup mayonnaise

¼ cup snipped chives

1 tsp kosher salt, more or less to taste

¼ tsp freshly ground black pepper

1 cup (or more to taste) fresh wild Maine blueberries

**Makes approximately 1 quart of potato salad**

Place potatoes in pot and completely cover with cold water. Bring to boil, reduce heat to a gentle simmer and cook potatoes until they still hold their shape but are tender when pierced with a sharp knife. Drain well in a colander and cool to room temperature.

Whisk together the yogurt, mayonnaise, chives, salt and pepper.

Toss cooled potatoes in sauce to coat. Gently fold in blueberries.

Chill until serving.

# Maggie's Black, White & Red Bean Salad

*Have you ever been invited to a murder mystery dinner party? Some years back, I was invited to one in Sunshine. The setting was perfect in Kelly's big Victorian house by the sea. I was to come dressed as a gypsy fortune teller and bring a dish of food for everyone to share. What a riot!! There were at least 20 of us all dressed up and playing a part. I think I spent more time laughing than trying to figure out who did the killing. What I do remember was sitting down to dinner and eating this delicious bean salad. Maggie happened to be sitting next to me dressed as a flapper girl and said she made it. There is nothing like it on a hot summers day and it is the perfect thing to bring to a pot luck supper.*

1 cup cooked black beans or one 15oz. can black beans, rinsed

1 cup cooked dried or frozen black eye peas

1 cup cooked small red kidney beans, or 1 15-oz. can red kidney beans, rinsed

1 medium cucumber, chopped

1 red bell pepper chopped

2 small carrots finely chopped

¼ cup chopped onion

¼ cup chopped parsley

### Dressing:

½ cup rice vinegar

1/3 cup olive oil

½ tsp salt

½ tsp granulated garlic

Black pepper to taste

### Serves 6 to 8

Combine all ingredients in a large bowl.

Whisk dressing ingredients together and stir into bean mixture.

Allow salad to marinate 1 hour at room temperature before serving.

# Crabmeat Potstickers

*Crabs are mostly what we catch as a by-product of lobster fishing, and their sweet meat has become a favorite of mine. Just tossed with some mayonnaise it is a staple on our summer picnic menus. These potstickers are a special treat when I have some extra time.*

1 pound red potatoes

1 tsp sea salt

1 pound crabmeat, picked through for shells

1 bunch scallions, chopped

¼ cup grated carrot

1 inch piece of fresh ginger, minced or grated

2 Tbls soy sauce or Tamari

2 tsps toasted sesame oil

Juice of 1 lemon

Pinch of cayenne pepper

1 package wonton wrappers

Water and or chicken stock

Canola or grapeseed oil for frying

Quarter the potatoes and place in a small pot. Cover with cold water, add salt and bring to a boil. Simmer potatoes until tender and drain. Leave potatoes in pot and set over low heat to cook off any remaining water. This takes just a few minutes, don't brown the potatoes. Remove from heat and mash. Let cool to room temperature. Add crabmeat, scallions, carrot, ginger, soy, sesame oil, lemon and pepper to potatoes. Mix gently until well blended.

To make potstickers: lay out a few wrappers at a time so they don't dry out. Place about 1 ½ teaspoons of filling in the center of each wrapper. With a pastry brush, dipped in water, brush the edges of the wrapper ( this is to help the wrapper stick together). Fold the wrapper diagonally, corner to corner and crimp the dumpling together in 4-5 pleated folds. Place on tray and cover with damp cloth while you finish making the rest.

**Makes 50 potstickers**

Heat 2 Tablespoons of oil in a skillet that has a tight fitting lid. Cooking in batches, place enough pot stickers in pan to cover with some room in between each one. Let cook, without disturbing, over medium high heat until bottoms of the dumplings have turned deep brown and stuck to the pan. VERY CAREFULLY pour in 1 cup of water or chicken stock. IT WILL SPLATTER. Quickly cover the pan and reduce heat to low. Cook covered until wrappers have softened and filling is heated through, 5-7 minutes.

Spoon dumplings onto platter and repeat process until all are cooked.

These are great by themselves or with your favorite dipping sauce.

# Lobster with Chervil, Nasturtium &
## sherry cream over brown rice pasta

*Nasturtiums grow everywhere on the island. One year I put nasturtium seeds in the planter boxes under the windows of our house on Greenhead and by August they had become so big they pulled the boxes off their brackets. The flowers are pretty and the whole plant is edible. They add a peppery flavor and great color to this dish. Pasta made with brown rice instead of durum wheat is lighter and goes better with the richness of the seafood.*

12 ounces brown rice linguine

1 pound fresh lobster meat
(approximately 2 1¼ lb. lobsters)

1 Tbls olive oil

½ cup diced red onion

½ cup dry sherry

2 cups clam juice or fish stock

⅓ cup chopped fresh chervil
(substitute 2 Tbls fresh tarragon if
chervil is not available)

½ cup chopped nasturtium flowers
with a few leaves added in

1 cup cream (I have successfully
substituted unsweetened soy milk)

Salt and pepper to taste

**Serves 4**

Bring a large pot of salted water to a boil. Cook pasta in water, stirring often until al dente, about 7 minutes. Drain pasta and toss with a bit of olive oil to keep it from sticking together. Set aside.

Heat oil over medium high heat in a large skillet, not non-stick. Add onions and saute, until just tender, about 3 minutes. Add sherry, bring to a boil and reduce liquid by ½, about 3 minutes. Add stock, chervil and nasturtiums, bring back to boil. Cook for a few minutes, add cream, bring to a boil and cook until sauce begins to thicken, about 4 minutes. Add lobster and continue cooking until lobster is heated through, about 2 minutes. Season with salt and pepper. Serve over pasta.

VARIATION
Toss lobster meat with chopped chervil, nasturtiums, onion and a pinch of fresh dill. Add ½ cup peeled, seeded and diced cucumber and enough mayonnaise to hold the salad together. Season with salt and pepper. Serve right away, the cucumber tends to make the salad watery if held too long.

# Mussels Three Different Ways

*One summer I cooked so many mussels so many different ways that we used to joke I could write a book just on ways to cook mussels. Here are the top three favorites. A green salad and some bread to sop up the delicious pan juice makes the perfect summer meal.*

## Mussels steamed in white wine and garlic

Place 1 ½ pounds of rope raised mussels in a large skillet. Add ½ cup white wine, 4 cloves of garlic, sliced and ¼ cup fresh basil leaves.

Cover pan and bring to a boil. Reduce heat and cook mussels over medium low heat until shells open and meat looks plump, but pulled from the shell.

## Mussels steamed in coconut milk and curry

Place 1 ½ pounds rope raised mussels in a large skillet. Add ¼ cup chopped scallions, ½ cup canned unsweetened coconut milk, 1 tsp curry powder, ¼ tsp or to taste of chili paste or good pinch of red pepper flakes. I grow lemon balm at the café and put a few leaves of that in too when I have it.

Cover pan and cook as directed in white wine and garlic version.

## Mussels a la Jambalaya

Place 1 ½ pounds of rope raised mussels in large skillet. Heat 1 Tbls oil over medium high heat in a large skillet. Add ¼ cup chopped fennel bulb, 2 cloves of garlic chopped and ½ cup diced Andouille or Chorizo sausage. Saute until fennel just softens and sausage begins to brown. Add 1 ½ pound rope raised mussels to skillet along with ¾ cup diced tomatoes and a ¼ cup white wine. Cover pan and cook mussels as directed in white wine and garlic version. These are best served over rice.

**Each Recipe Serves 2**

# Pan Seared Tuna Steak
## with garlic & wasabi sour cream

*If you overcook tuna it is dry and chewy. Cooked properly it is moist, tender and delicious. Since tuna steak usually comes fairly large, I like to cut it into thick chunks, marinate it and pan sear it golden brown on the outside, leaving the center looking like a perfectly cooked medium rare steak.*

3 pounds fresh tuna, cut into 1 ½ inch cubes

2 Tbls olive oil

2 tsp toasted sesame oil

¼ cup tamari

1 Tbls rice wine vinegar

½ tsp grated lemon peel

¼ cup fresh basil leaves, ripped

¼ cup chopped fresh cilantro

4-5 cloves garlic, chopped

Crushed red pepper flakes to taste

¾ cup sour cream

¼ tsp wasabi powder

**Serves 4-6**

Combine oils, tamari, vinegar, lemon peel, herbs, garlic and red pepper flakes in a large bowl. Add cubed tuna and marinate for 30 minutes at room temperature.

Meanwhile whisk together the sour cream and wasabi and set aside.

Heat a cast iron skillet over high heat until very hot. It will smoke lightly when ready.

Add tuna in batches leaving an inch between cubes. Sear on each side until nicely browned, about 1 ½ - 2 minutes total.

Serve over rice with wasabi sour cream and slices of ripe tomato.

# Sauted Cabbage with Tomato Sauce
## & smoked mozzarella cheese

*It is amazing to me how trends seep their way into every nook and cranny of our existence. Uneaten bread filled the compost pile last summer from customers avoiding carbs and I failed to have a dinner party that didn't include someone on the Atkins or South Beach diet. On a whim, I put this main course together one night and fell in love with it. As odd as it sounds, the cabbage makes a wonderful substitute for the traditional role pasta plays in this dish. Sometimes when I am feeling really decadent I will add some Italian sausage or Pancetta.*

3 Tbls olive oil

1 medium head of white cabbage, cored and sliced thinly

½ cup white wine

Salt and pepper to taste

4 ounce ball smoked mozzarella cheese, cut into ½-inch cubes

2 cups quality jarred or homemade tomato sauce

Heat oil in a large skillet over medium high heat. Add cabbage and saute until crisp tender, about 15 minutes. Season with salt and pepper. Add wine, bring to a boil and simmer until just a few tablespoons of liquid remains. Stir in tomato sauce and cook until heated through, about 10 minutes. Adjust seasoning. Stir in cubes of cheese. Serve piping hot.

TIP: If you are using sausage or pancetta, saute it first in the olive oil and then add cabbage and continue with recipe.

**Serves 4**

# Grilled Turkey Burgers

*I love to see the island through the eyes of our friends' grandchildren. Living full time in the city, both boys seem to really look forward to their visit and call the month that they spend on Deer Isle "Camp Grandma and Grandpa." They play ball in the huge field next to their grandparents' house, dig potatoes from the garden, fish on a dock in the harbor and take turns on the riding lawn mower. Last 4th of July, Janice set up a beautiful table under the trees with a centerpiece of huge peonies. We played badminton while the burgers were cooking and finished the meal with homemade peach ice cream. Truly a day to remember.*

2 pounds ground turkey (a mixture of light and dark meat makes the moistest burger)

2 Tbls dijon mustard

1 medium onion, minced

4 cloves garlic, minced

½ cup grated apple

¼ cup chopped fresh basil

2 tsp kosher salt or to taste

½ tsp ground black pepper

**Makes 8 burgers**

Place all ingredients together in a bowl. Mix gently but firmly to distribute seasonings throughout the meat. Don't ovemix or the burgers will be rubbery.

Shape into 8 burger patties.

Grill over medium hot coals until cooked through in the center and nicely browned on the outside.

Great with fresh tomato, cheese, relish, you name it.

# Gluten Free Yellow Cake with Berries

*The whole island is veined with old wood roads from many years ago. Cleared as a path for loggers and other workers, they offer an intricate passageway through most of the dense woods that surround us. Over the past 10 years ATV's have become a popular recreational vehicle. Often the riders use these old wood roads and have enabled me to walk them without much interference. Following one of these secret paths I discovered a huge wild blueberry field surrounded by Fir trees. Every summer, with the land owners permission, I plop myself down amongst the bees and dragonflys to fill a bucket or two of the sweet juicy berries. This basic yellow cake, moist and tender and gluten free, is the perfect thing to fold them into.*

 Gluten Free

 Sugar Free

2 ¼ cups brown rice flour

¼ cup sweet brown rice flour

½ cup tapioca flour

1 ½ Tbls baking powder

½ tsp salt

½ cup light vegetable oil, sunflower, almond, safflower, etc.

¾ cup brown rice syrup, GF

¼ cup maple syrup

1½ cups soy milk or regular milk

1 tsp pure vanilla extract, GF

2 cups fresh blueberries, raspberries or blackberries

**Makes 12 servings**

Preheat oven to 350 degrees. Lightly grease a 9" x 13" pan with oil or oil spray.

Whisk together the flours, baking powder and salt in a large bowl. In another bowl whisk together the oil, syrups, soy milk and vanilla. Mix the wet ingredients into the dry and stir until well blended and thick. Fold in berries. Pour into prepared pan and bake until toothpick in center comes out with a few dry crumbs attached. Cool completely before serving, approximately 25-30 minutes.

VARIATION
Omit the berries and bake in two 9" round cake pans and you have the base for a wonderful yellow layer cake. Smear layers with jam, fresh fruit, sweetened Greek Yogurt or use the almond cream frosting recipe on page 39.

# Oatmeal Raisin Cookies

*Surely I would have been lynched by my customers if I had left this recipe out of my book.*
*Everybody loves these things!!*
*These cookies are a meal in themselves and many people buy them at the café for a snack while kayaking.*
*Since I don't make them everyday, some of the more desperate addicts buy six at a time and ask if they will keep.*
*Several years ago Renee and I went to England. I had packed some snacks for the long plane ride, and somehow one of these cookies ended up in the bottom of my backpack, all but forgotten until packing 10 days later to return home. Always seizing the moment, we decided to make tea and enjoy the cookie. It was delicious!!*

1 ⅓ cups softened unsalted butter

1 ¾ cups packed brown sugar

2 medium eggs

2 Tbls honey

¾ tsp salt

1 Tbls pure vanilla extract

7 ½ cups rolled oats

2 cups unbleached all purpose flour

1 cup raisins

**Makes 12 very large cookies**

Preheat your oven to 350 degrees.

Place the flour, oats and raisins in a large bowl.

Beat the butter and sugar with a mixer until just creamy. Add the eggs, honey, salt and vanilla and beat to combine. Add the butter mixture to the flour mixture and with your hands (take your rings off) mix the dough together until all is moist and will hold together.

Form the dough into 12 cookies the size of baseballs. Wet your hands to do this or the dough will stick to you unmercifully. Place the cookies on a lightly greased tray. Flatten each one to an inch thickness.

Bake for about 15 minutes or until the desired color of golden brown that suits you.

Remove from oven and allow to cool.

# Chocolate Chocolate Cookies with Nuts

*Every good café has a version of these decadent cookies on the counter.*

1 cup good (we use Guittard) semi-sweet chocolate chips

2 ounces unsweetened chocolate, chopped

6 Tbls unsalted butter

2 eggs

1 ½ Tbls instant espresso powder

1 ½ tsp pure vanilla extract

¾ cup sugar

6 Tbls unbleached all purpose flour

1 tsp baking powder

½ tsp salt

1 cup roughly chopped walnuts

1 cup roughly chopped pecans

1 cup good semi-sweet chocolate chips

**Makes 15 cookies**

Preheat oven to 325 degrees.

Melt 1 cup chocolate chips, unsweetened chocolate and butter in microwave or over a double boiler on the stove. Stir until smooth. Don't overheat chocolate or it will burn.

Combine eggs, espresso powder and vanilla in large bowl. Beat until combined. Add sugar and beat until thick and creamy. Add chocolate and mix well. Whisk together the flour, baking powder and salt in a separate bowl. Fold into chocolate mixture until dry ingredients are moist. Add nuts and remaining cup of chocolate chips folding them in to distribute evenly.

Using a ¼ cup ice cream scoop or heaping tablespoons, drop cookies onto parchment lined baking trays, 2 inches apart. Bake 6 minutes, turn trays and bake another 4-6 minutes more. You want the tops to be cracked, but the inside of the cookie to still be gooey. Remove from oven, cool 10 minutes on baking tray and then remove them to racks to cool completely.

# Blueberry Layer Cake
## with cream cheese frosting

*Nothing hits you in the eye like a three tier white cake speckled all over with tiny Maine blueberries and thick cream cheese frosting.*
*Pure comfort food.*

2 sticks plus 2 tablespoons unsalted butter at room temperature

2¼ cups sugar

5 large eggs separated

2 teaspoons vanilla

3½ cups cake flour

1 teaspoon baking powder

½ teaspoon salt

1 cup milk at room temperature

2 cups fresh or frozen wild Maine blueberries

Preheat oven to 350 degrees. Grease and flour three 9" round cake pans

Cream the butter and sugar with an electric mixer until light and fluffy (about 5 minutes). With the mixer on medium speed add the egg yolks one at a time, beating until each is incorporated before adding the next. Add the vanilla.

Whisk or sift together the flour, baking powder and salt.

With the mixer on low speed add flour and milk alternately in three batches, beginning and ending with the flour.

In another bowl, whip the egg whites until they are just stiff. Don't overmix or they will become dry and so will the cake.

Gently fold the egg whites into the batter and then the blueberries. If frozen berries are used, fold the blueberries in with just a few turns so the juice doesn't turn your batter blue.

Divide cake batter into the prepared pans. Bake for 25-35 minutes or until toothpick inserted into center of cake comes out clean.

Let cool almost completely in pans and then remove cakes from pans onto wire racks *When completely cool frost and serve.*

*NOTE: This cake keeps well in the refrigerator up to 4 days.*

## Cream Cheese Frosting

1 ½ - 2 sticks of butter at room temperature

1 pound of cream cheese, softened

4 cups powdered sugar

1 teaspoon lemon juice

**Makes enough to frost a three layer cake**

Beat butter and cream cheese with electric mixer until very creamy. On low speed add powdered sugar 1 cup at a time until incorporated.

Add lemon juice and beat frosting on high until light and fluffy, or desired consistency.

# Fall

*Each autumn it feels like i get to discover my home all over again ...*

# Pumpkin Cream Cheese Muffins

*One morning about 5 years ago I was headed to work and saw the answering machine blinking. As usual I was in a hurry and didn't stop to check it. About an hour later Renee called to tell me I had better call my Mother in Florida. My Father had died suddenly from a heart attack while getting ready for bed. Needless to say my whole world went upside down for a while. You always hear how small towns pull together in times of crisis. Well, they do. People couldn't have been nicer or more supportive. Cards, offers to fill in at the café, stories of similar circumstances. Truly, my community helped me through a very hard time.*

*My Mother is now 45 minutes away in a nursing home in Ellsworth and she loves it. The staff is so nice that I try to bring a special treat every so often. When I have let too much time pass in between treats they ask for these muffins by name.*

1 cup pureed pumpkin (I use canned pumpkin unless I happen to have fresh on hand in the fall)

2 large eggs

½ cup light oil

⅓ cup milk

1 ½ cups sugar

1 ½ cups unbleached all purpose flour

1 tsp salt

¾ tsp cinnamon

¼ tsp ground ginger

½ tsp nutmeg

a pinch of clove

1 tsp baking soda

**Filling**
4 ounces cream cheese at room temperature, ¼ cup sugar, 1 tsp vanilla

**Makes 12 muffins**

Preheat oven to 350 degrees.

Grease 12 muffin cups

In a large bowl whisk together the pumpkin, eggs, oil, milk and 1 ½ cups sugar until smooth. Add the flour, salt, spices and baking soda. Stir just until well combined.

Divide batter among the 12 greased muffin cups.

In a small bowl combine the cream cheese, ¼ cup sugar and vanilla. Beat until smooth and creamy.

Stuff a spoonful of the cream cheese mixture into the middle of each cup of muffin batter. Let the cream cheese stay nestled in the batter, not covered over.

Bake muffins for 20 – 25 minutes until puffed and the cream cheese is golden. I sometimes stick a toothpick in the center of the muffin next to the cream cheese and if it comes out clean the muffins are done. Allow to cool in pan for 15 minutes and then remove them to a platter to cool completely.

NOTE: At the café and when I give these as gifts around the holidays I double the recipe and make 14-15 big muffins.

# Curried Pumpkin Soup

*Every autumn season I find myself driving away from the water towards the rolling farmland that lies just a bit beyond my home by the sea. Visions of apples and pumpkins dance in my head..*

*With empty boxes in the back of my car I head straight for the Johnston Apple Orchard located just outside Ellsworth on Rte 1A. An old family farm, over 500 apple trees stand nestled in a valley surrounded by hills and fields. Two years ago they introduced me to Honey Crisp apples which are now my favorite eating apple. This year they had a beautiful crop of early Paula Reds, a favorite of mine for apple pie.*

*With my boxes loaded I head up the road a ways to Annie's Pride Farm Stand. "Mr. Annie" (I've never asked him his name) grows a plethora of pumpkins and squash. This year I fell in love with the Long Island Cheese pumpkin. He promises me it makes the best pumpkin pie. We'll see.*

*Meandering home I follow hand made signs to old barns, always with a cat or two, making sure that I put my money in the can for the small bounty I discover.*

*When I finally arrive back on the island, I'm pretty sure everyone knows what the soup will be tomorrow.*

TIP: Canned pumpkin is perfectly wonderful in this soup, Libby is my favorite. But if you find that perfect pumpkin or squash that you are dying to taste, this is what we do in the café to get nice thick puree easily.

Cut the pumpkin in half, scoop out the seeds and lay cut side down on a baking tray. Add just a bit of water to keep it moist.

Bake at 350 degrees until tender, about 20 –30 minutes depending on the size. Let it cool to a temperature you can handle and scoop the flesh out of the skins.

At this point you can either puree the pumpkin in a food processor or add it to the soup and use a blender wand on the whole soup to get a nice consistency.

4 tablespoons butter or sunflower oil

2 stalks celery, chopped

1 medium to large onion, chopped

1 medium apple peeled, cored and chopped

2 tablespoons flour

2 tablespoons curry

4 cups chicken or vegetable stock

3 whole cloves

1 stick of cinnamon

¾ teaspoon salt

12 cups pureed or canned pumpkin

1 cup half and half

**Serves 6-8 as first course
4 as main course**

Melt butter or oil in a medium soup pot. Add celery, onion and apple and sauté until tender.

Stir in flour and then curry. Cook for 2 minutes stirring constantly. Pour in stock and stir until smooth.

Add salt, cloves and cinnamon stick (If you are doubling or tripling this soup for a crowd, you may want to wrap the cloves and cinnamon in cheesecloth so you can easily remove it when the soup is through cooking.) Bring to boil and simmer 30 minutes uncovered. Remove the cloves and cinnamon and whisk in the pumpkin puree. Bring back to simmer and then stir in the half and half. Season with pepper and salt to taste.

# Smoked Haddock Chowder
## with sweet potato & bacon

*I feel like I moved here right at the end of the " good old days". Akin to looking at a faded picture, with some of its image still clear, I feel like I have glimpsed life here long ago. Enough of that image still exists that changes to it can cut deep. For years and years there had been an overgrown swamp across from where I live. The sugar maples turned brilliant orange-red in the fall and even though we live right on the main road, you could still look out the window and see a woodland. For better or for worse a Seafood Processing Plant now stands in the middle of the swamp. In a couple of years the hedge we planted will blot out the building, but I rely on the smoked haddock they sell to make this delicious chowder.*

¼ pound of bacon, diced

I red onion, diced

2-3 cloves garlic, chopped

⅓ cup sherry

2 medium sweet potatoes, peeled and cut into ½ " cubes

4 cups mussel or clam juice

I cup cream

I can evaporated milk

I pound smoked haddock

Salt and pepper to taste

Pinch of fresh sage and a sprig of thyme

In a medium sized soup pot cook bacon over medium heat until browned and with a slotted spoon remove to paper towels to drain.

Pour off all but I tablespoon of bacon fat and cook onion in remaining fat until it begins to turn translucent and soften. Add garlic and cook 2 minutes. Add sherry, turn up heat and reduce the liquid by half, scraping up the brown bits on the bottom of the pot. Stir in sweet potatoes. Add stock, bring to a boil, turn heat to simmer and cook until potatoes are just tender. Stir in cream, evaporated milk, haddock and bacon. Season with salt and pepper. Stir over low heat just until cream heats up. Turn off heat, if you have the fresh herbs throw them in. Cover the pot and let the chowder stand I hour before serving. Adjust seasoning.

**Serves 4 as a main course**

# Fresh Crabmeat Salad in a Wrap
## with grape tomatoes & greens

*The month of September on the Island is magic.*
*A very kind woman gave four of us permission to walk out to her island at low tide and enjoy a picnic anywhere we chose. The house was unoccupied so we chose a second story deck overlooking the autumn landscape and water beyond. I will never forget that day. The sun was shining, we were the only ones on earth and we had brought some awesome picnic fare. These sandwiches seemed the perfect balance of elegance and simplicity that described the day.*

I pound fresh crabmeat

¼ cup mayonnaise

¼ - ½ tsp sweet smoked paprika

I Tbls fresh lemon juice

Fresh lettuce leaves

½ pint grape tomatoes, sliced in half lengthwise

Package of 8" flour tortillas

Gently toss the crabmeat, mayonnaise, paprika and lemon juice together until combined.

Place a handful of lettuce in center of each wrap top lettuce with ¼ cup of crabmeat or as much as you like, sprinkle with tomatoes. Fold the left and right side of the wrap toward the middle and then roll it up from the bottom. Serve on a platter or wrap individually for a picnic lunch. Keep chilled until served.

**Serves 8**

VARIATIONS
1. Substitute curry for the paprika and add cucumbers to the wrap.
2. Serve sandwiches open face on toasted bread.

# Green Salad with Grilled Chicken,
## honeyed peaches & feta cheese

*Dr. Ostertag saved my Mother's life. As appreciative of that as I am, I am equally grateful for her gardening skills. She has an extraordinary green thumb and has turned me on to many of life's great pleasures. Like Sungold tomatoes. Little orange jewels that are like little packets of sweetness that burst in your mouth. And her peaches! Last September she came by the café with a box full of them. We traded peaches for chocolate cake and I couldn't have been happier. I made pies, and cobbler. I sliced and froze some to enjoy in the middle of January and the best thing I did with them was make this salad for dinner.*

4 cups fresh (in season) peaches, pitted and cut into ½ inch pieces

½ cup of a delicious dry red wine

⅓ cup honey

1 tsp five spice powder

½ cup fresh basil leaves, julienned

½ tsp sea salt

Freshly ground black pepper

4-6 grilled boneless breasts of chicken

Creamy Feta cheese

Mesclun salad mix

Place the peaches, wine, honey, five spice powder and basil in a bowl and stir to combine. Season with salt and freshly ground pepper to taste. Let this mixture macerate for 1 hour at room temperature.

When ready to serve, place greens on each person's plate, top with slices of grilled chicken. Spoon the peaches over the chicken and top with feta cheese. Drizzle extra virgin olive oil over the salad and season with salt and pepper to taste.

NOTE: This salad is delicious with grilled pork tenderloin. Also, try using a slightly fruity white wine like a Riesling for a slightly different flavor with the peaches.

**Serves 6**

# Potato Custard Tart with Tomato,
## onion & parmesan cheese

*I don't think I have ever been to potlucks like the ones I have been to on this island. Potluck suppers, potluck birthday parties, potluck picnics and I have been to two potluck weddings. Local baby showers are a phenomenon unto themselves. Never is there less than 60 people. The presents are mounded to the ceiling and the food spreads across the entire room. I never know what to bring. Everything is there from artichoke dip to cream puffs and it is always good.*

*This tart is elegant, yet easy to put together. It works hot or at room temperature.*

1 Tbls olive oil

1 Tbls butter

2 cloves garlic, chopped

1-2 pounds red potatoes, sliced very thinly

2-3 large ripe tomatoes, cut into ¼-inch slices

1 medium yellow onion, peeled, cut in half and cut into thin slices

1+ cups freshly grated parmesan cheese

1 Tbls chopped fresh thyme or marjoram

4 eggs

⅓ cup cream

Salt and pepper to taste

Preheat oven to 350 degrees.

Warm oil and butter in shallow baking pan until butter is melted. Sprinkle with ½ the chopped garlic.

Cover the bottom of the dish with an overlapping layer of sliced potatoes. Stand potato slices up around the edge to form a side crust. Sprinkle with remaining ½ of garlic, salt and pepper to taste. Cover potatoes with ½ of parmesan cheese. Cover cheese layer with a layer of onion and a tight layer of tomato slices, don't overlap them. Season lightly with salt, pepper and herbs. Cover with another thick layer of parmesan cheese. Whisk eggs and a pinch of salt until foamy, whisk in cream. Pour evenly over tomatoes.

Cover dish with foil and bake for 30 minutes or until potatoes are tender. Uncover and bake until custard is set and top is golden brown, 15 more minutes.

**Serves 6-8**

# Sticky Rice with Turkey Sausage
## & dried cranberries

*Thanksgiving is my favorite holiday. No gifts, just a table full of food and, hopefully, lots of people to share it with. Last Thanksgiving was extra special. We were invited to an afternoon meal with our friends who own Edgewood Farm. It was a classic affair set in a lovely big old farmhouse kitchen. A whole bunch of us ate around a huge table, laughing and telling stories. Best of all, I didn't have to do any cooking. Then around 8'oclock that evening my Aunt called to invite me up for turkey sandwiches. Minutes later I was sitting at their table slathering the mayo on my gluten free bread, giggling and eating some more delicious turkey that I didn't have to cook. Getting into bed that night I really felt that I had a lot to be thankful for.*

*This rice dish is a wonderful gluten free addition to any holiday table.*

2 cups sweet brown rice

Cold water to cover

2 Tbls oil

½ cup diced red onion

1 lb. of your favorite sausage, diced
(I use a local chicken sausage)

½ cup diced carrots

⅓ cup dry sherry

3 cups chicken stock

¾ cup sliced green onion

½ - ¾ cup chopped dried cranberries

Put the rice in a bowl and cover with cold water. Let soak for 2 hours. Drain and rinse.

In a heavy bottom pot, heat the oil. Add the onion and sauté for 5 minutes until just starting to get tender. Add carrots and sausage, cook 2 more minutes. Add sherry, bring to a boil and reduce liquid by half.

Stir in drained rice and then stir in stock. Bring to a boil, reduce heat to low and cook covered until rice is tender and the liquid has been absorbed approximately 40 minutes. Remove cover and stir in green onions and cranberries with a fork. Cover and let stand 10 minutes before serving.

**Serves 8 as a side dish**

# Homemade Sausage Patties
## with turkey or pork

*Everyone always asked me, "How in the world do you come up with the things you come up with?" This recipe is a perfect entreé into my crazy food brain:*

*It is 11 am on Saturday and I'm starting to get really hungry. In the freezer I find a package of ground turkey we bought at the Common Ground Fair; 25 minutes to defrost in some luke warm water. Yesterday my Aunt gave me leeks and carrots from her garden.*

*I still have fresh sage in my garden , dried cranberries in the cupboard and one Cameo apple left from a farmers market in Boston last weekend.*

*Scrambled eggs and homemade sausage!!*

*Sausage is the easiest thing to make and takes little time. Use ground turkey or pork and let your imagination flow.*

2 –3 medium leeks, cut in half length wise, sliced and run under cold water to wash

1 small to medium carrot grated

1 small apple peeled, cored and grated (dice if the apple is a soft variety)

2 or 3 tablespoons dried cranberries, chopped

1 pound ground pork or turkey

2 tablespoons chopped fresh sage

Pinch of dried or fresh thyme

1 clove garlic minced

Salt and pepper to taste

**Serves 4-6**

Saute leeks in 2 tablespoons oil under tender. In bowl combine all ingredients until blended. (Don't overmix or sausage will become tough). Form into 2 inch patties.

Coat bottom of heavy bottom skillet (I like cast iron) with oil. Brown sausage patties in skillet until nicely brown on both sides and cooked through.

# Turkey Roulade

*Just around the corner and down the road a piece from the café sits a sweet little farm that raises turkeys at Thanksgiving. Around October you can drive by and see hundreds and hundreds of turkeys clucking about.*

*Often I see people taking pictures of the boat in the grass engulfed by white birds with the old barn in the background. Sometimes just after the holiday, if they have extra, I can get my hands on some boneless breasts of turkey. I love to make this roulade and invite people over for a casual supper and maybe a card game or two.*

¼ cup olive oil

4 cloves of garlic, chopped fine

1 boneless breast of turkey
2 – 2 ½ pounds

4 ounces of goat cheese

½ cup fresh basil leaves, julienned

⅓ cup diced sundried tomatoes

½ bunch scallions, sliced thin

Dash of crushed red pepper flakes

Salt and pepper to taste

**Serves 6-8**

Preheat oven to 400 degrees.

Whisk the oil and garlic together to blend. Set aside.

Place turkey breast skin side up between two pieces of plastic wrap. With a meat mallet (I use the flat side of a hammer) pound out the breast to ½-inch thickness. You should end up with a 9" x12" irregular looking rectangle.

Remove the top sheet of plastic wrap and brush turkey with most of the olive oil, saving a bit to rub on the outside of the rolled turkey breast. Sprinkle with the basil, cheese, tomatoes and scallions, making sure to go all the way to the sides so the filling is evenly distributed. Sprinkle with red pepper and season with salt and pepper to taste.

Starting on 1 long side, roll up the breast jelly roll style and secure the edges together with a few tooth picks. Tie the body of the roulade with kitchen twine to keep it from unrolling while baking. Place roulade in a roasting pan lightly coated with oil. Brush turkey with remaining olive oil and sprinkle with salt and pepper.

Roast roulade until thermometer inserted in the thickest part registers 160, about 35 minutes.

Remove turkey from oven and let stand at room temperature for 5 minutes. Transfer to a cutting board and tent with foil while making sauce. Slice into ¾-inch slices, pour sauce over slices and serve hot or at room temperature.

**For Sauce**

½ cup chicken stock

¼ cup white wine

Place the baking pan with the turkey juice on burner. Add ½ cup chicken broth and ¼ cup white wine. Bring to boil, scraping up brown bits from bottom of pan and reduce liquid to a thin sauce consistency.

# Simply Delicious Chicken Wings

*I LOVE the game of football. I must admit that I didn't know if I could be a Patriots fan after rooting for the Bengals for so long. But, we have won three Super Bowls and Tom Brady is awfully cute. Both Renee and my cat hate when I watch the games at home. They say I yell too much. So I have spent many a Sunday afternoon on Janice and Roman's couch eating chicken wings and yelling to my heart's content.*

3 lbs chicken wings, joints split and the tip discarded

3 cloves of garlic, sliced

¾ cup dry red wine

¼ cup water

1 tsp sweet or hot smoked paprika

1 ½ Tbls sherry vinegar

2 tsp sugar (I use date sugar)

2 tsp sea salt

## Dipping Sauce

1 cup mayonnaise

1 tsp sherry

½ tsp smoked paprika (sweet or hot)

**Serves 4-6 as a main course or 8-10 as an appetizer**

Place the wings in a heavy plastic bag.

Whisk the remaining ingredients together and pour over chicken wings. Toss to coat and let wings marinate in the refrigerator 4 hours or overnight, turning occasionally.

Preheat oven to 400.

Line a baking tray with aluminum foil and place wings on tray in a single layer.

Roast until browned and cooked through, about 30 minutes.

If you want a crispy skin, put them under the broiler for 5 minutes before serving.

Whisk together and serve alongside wings.

VARIATION

For an Asian flavor use 5 spice powder instead of paprika and soy sauce instead of sherry vinegar in the marinade. I also add 5 or 6 thin slices of fresh ginger.

For the dipping sauce I use ground coriander instead of the paprika and add a bit of fresh cilantro.

# Chicken Braised with Shitake Mushrooms,
## pancetta & sage

*My friends Duncan and Edward have a beautiful house on the water in Deer Isle. I just love being invited over. I always wear a dress and pretend I am a princess away from her castle. The dining room always sparkles with interesting people and really good food.*

2 ¼" slices of Pancetta (Italian bacon), finely diced

1 chicken cut into 8 pieces

1 medium onion, chopped

1 head of garlic, sliced in half horizontally

1 cup red wine

½ cup chicken stock

1 ounce dried Shitake mushrooms

¾ cup hot water

1 ½ tsp dried sage, crumbled

Salt and pepper to taste

1 Tbls potato starch or flour

2 Tbls cold water

**Serves 4**

Place mushrooms in hot water and set aside to soak for 30 minutes.

Heat a large heavy bottomed skillet over medium heat and saute Pancetta until nicely browned. Remove from skillet to a bowl and set aside. Pour off all but 1 tablespoon of fat from the bacon. Brown the chicken pieces over medium high heat in the fat until a deep golden brown on both sides. Do this in batches so you don't overcrowd the chicken. You will get a nicer color and flavor. Place chicken on a plate and set aside.

Add onion and garlic and saute until onion is soft and translucent, about 10-15 minutes. Meanwhile, remove the stems from the mushrooms and slice them thinly. Save the water. When onions are soft add the mushrooms and red wine. Bring to boil and reduce liquid to a thickened sauce. Add chicken and pancetta back to skillet with the water from the mushrooms and the stock. You want the liquid to be half way up the sides of the chicken. You can add more stock if necessary. Season with sage, salt and pepper. Bring to a boil, reduce heat and simmer, covered, on low until chicken is tender, about 45 minutes to an hour. Remove chicken to a plate and tent with foil. Retrieve garlic halves and using a paper towel so you don't burn your fingers, squeeze the tender garlic from the skin into the pot, discarding the skins.

Bring the the liquid to a boil. Stir the starch into the cold water until a smooth paste forms, whisk into the liquid and stir until thickened. Taste for salt and pepper. Place the chicken in the sauce and serve.

# Roasted Autumn Vegetables
## over wild & brown rice with goat cheese

*The transition to summer on the island is intense. The island population swells to more than four times its year round size, people's attitudes are a bit different and expectations are high. There is so much to do; parties and events, people to see, a living to make. The months fly by. Suddenly there is an ad for the Blue Hill Fair, the sunlight's shadows are lower and it is time to settle down again for the 10 months ahead.*

I small head garlic

Olive oil

I small buttercup squash, peeled and cut into 1"pieces

I large red onion, peeled and cut into eighths

I medium eggplant, cut into 1" pieces

I head of broccoli, cut into florets and steamed until crisp tender

8 ounces mushrooms, quartered

I red bell pepper, seeded and cut into 1-inch pieces

2 Tbls chopped fresh parsley

2 Tbls chopped fresh rosemary

I Tbls chopped fresh thyme

Salt and pepper to taste

Preheat oven to 450 degrees.

Cut head of garlic in half, rub with oil, then wrap in foil and roast in oven along with vegetables until tender.

Toss the squash, onion and eggplant in a bowl with 2-3 tablespoons olive oil and sprinkle with salt and pepper. Spread in a single layer on a rimmed baking dish. Roast in oven for 20 – 25 minutes, turning occasionally, until tender and browned. Remove from oven.

Meanwhile, toss broccoli, red pepper and mushrooms together with 2-3 tablespoons olive oil and sprinkle with salt and pepper. Spread in a single layer on a rimmed baking dish. Roast in oven for 15-20 minutes, turning occasionally, until tender and golden. Remove from oven.

Toss all roasted vegetables together in a large bowl. Squeeze roasted garlic from skin and toss with vegetables. Season with fresh herbs and adjust salt and pepper.

I cup long grain brown rice

I cup wild rice

4 cups water or vegetable stock

2 Tbls butter

2 tsp salt

4 ounces creamy goat cheese

**Serves 4-6**

Place water or stock in a 2 qt. pot with a tight fitting lid. Add butter and salt. Bring to a boil, add rice, stir, reduce heat to low and cook covered without stirring for 45 minutes or until water is absorbed and rice is tender.

Serve vegetables over rice, drizzle with olive oil and top with crumbled goat cheese.

TIP: Please feel free to mix and match other autumn vegetables. Just roast them together according to similar times they take to become tender and golden in the oven.

# Spaghetti Squash with Leeks,
## apples & sausage

*I find autumn to be blissful all over Maine. The crowds are gone, the weather is gorgeous and the vegetables are still numerous. Squash is something that seems to grow quite prolifically here. In the midst of a rather slow evening at the Café I put some spaghetti squash in the oven to bake, really to see what all the fuss about this particular squash was all about. Upon taking it out of the oven and running a fork down the flesh, the golden strands of squash totally seduced me. Fresh leeks, apples, squash, the leaves all turning colors, and yes big heavy sweaters and walks in the woods. Those images of Fall in New England are definitely art imitating life.*

I spaghetti squash

I bunch of leeks, white and pale green part only

I large crisp apple, cored and diced

2 Tbls oil, sunflower or olive oil

½ pound of garlic roasted sausage or one of your favorite flavors available to you, diced

¼ tsp dried thyme or ¾ tsp fresh thyme leaves, chopped

¼ cup sherry (optional)

Salt and pepper to taste

**Serves 4**

Preheat oven to 350 degrees.

Cut squash in half lengthwise and scoop out seeds. Place flesh sides down on a lightly oiled baking tray and bake in oven until flesh is very tender. A fork should slide into the flesh through the skin very easily.

Remove squash from oven. When cool enough to handle without burning your hands scrape the flesh from the skin with a fork. The squash should just naturally form long thin strands that look like spaghetti. Set aside.

Heat I tablespoon of oil in large heavy bottomed skillet over medium heat. Add sausage and cook until lightly browned. Remove from skillet to a bowl. Reduce heat to low and add the remaining oil and leeks to the same skillet. Cook until leeks are tender, about 10 – 15 minutes. Add apple and thyme to skillet and saute until apple just starts to get soft but still has some firmness to it, about 5-8 minutes depending on the variety of apple. Return the sausage to the skillet and, if you are using sherry, add it to the pan now and reduce the liquid, scraping up any brown bits on the bottom of the skillet. This just takes a few minutes. The sherry will be mostly gone. Add the squash to the pan and heat through, stirring to combine all the ingredients. Season with salt and pepper.

# Lily's Nutburgers

*The original moments of these wonderful burgers made from nuts, cheese and brown rice are really planted in my first restaurant in Cincinnati. That is where they came alive. But their life, like mine, really opened up and became full when they got to Maine. The original recipe was published in my first cookbook which is no longer in print. I have had more requests for this recipe than any other. Since they are as much a part of my life now as they were then, I felt it appropriate to include them in these moments.*

*The key to the success of these burgers is a bit of extra water in the rice and the addition of the rice when it is hot from the pan. So don't make the rice ahead of time thinking you can put the burgers together later on in the day.*

½ cup long grain brown rice

1 ¼ cups water

1 Tbls unsalted butter

1 tsp salt

7 ounces unsalted cashews

7 ounces walnuts

1 cup shredded cheddar cheese

1 Tbls chili powder

¾ tsp dried basil

¾ tsp dried oregano

¾ tsp paprika

¼ tsp cayenne pepper, or to taste

1 tsp salt

½ tsp black pepper

**Makes 8-10 burgers**

In a small pot with a tight fitting lid, place the rice, water, butter and 1 tsp of salt. Bring to a boil, stir, cover and reduce heat to low. Cook 45 minutes without stirring. The rice should be tender and a bit of water should be left in the bottom of the pot.

While the rice is cooking place the nuts in the bowl of a food processor and grind them to a fine meal. Place them in a large bowl along with the remaining ingredients.

When the rice is done, add it to the nut mixture and combine thoroughly without overworking it or it will get mealy.

Form into 8 – 10 patties and let cool.

Heat a heavy bottom non stick skillet and coat the bottom with oil (we use canola). Place the burgers in batches in the hot pan and cook until well browned on each side.

We serve them on crusty bread with mayo, mustard, lettuce, tomato and sprouts.

They are very hardy and freeze well if you wish to make a batch to have on hand.

# Porcini Dusted Pork Chops
## over mushroom polenta

*Pungent earth from the woods, the aroma of dried porcini mushrooms completely seduces me. Soaking them and adding them to stews, braises and sauces is a sure bet to a complex flavor, but I couldn't help wondering what it would be like to use them all ground up like a powder and put directly on something. These pork chops were my first experiment and there is another recipe in this book for chicken fingers that call for the dust to be added to the bread crumbs. Use a spice grinder or a small bowled food processor to get the finest ground powder. The smell and the added flavor is superior.*

### Pork Chops

4 1½-inch thick pork chops with bone

or without

1 ounce dried porcini mushrooms,

divided in half

Hot water

Salt

Pepper

Dried sage

Dried thyme

Dried rosemary

1 Tbls olive oil

3 shallots, peeled and diced or 1 small

red onion

½ cup sherry

2-3 cups chicken stock

Pat the chops dry with a paper towel and lay out on a tray. Puree half of the dried mushrooms to a fine powder and soak the other half in hot water to cover until soft. Rub equal amounts of mushroom powder on both sides of each pork chop. Then sprinkle with salt, pepper, sage, thyme and rosemary to taste.

Cover chops and let stand at room temperature for 30 mintues, or in the fridge for 2 hours.

Preheat oven to 350 degrees.

Heat oil over medium high heat in a large heavy bottomed skillet (cast iron works the best for this) Add the seasoned pork chops and brown well on both sides, about 6-8 minutes per side. Remove from pan and set aside.

Add shallots to skillet and stir until browned, about 4 minutes. While the onions are browning, remove the soaking mushrooms from the water and chop, set the mushrooms aside for the polenta and save the soaking water. When the onions are golden brown add sherry to pan to deglaze, scraping up any brown bits on the bottom of the skillet. Simmer for two minutes.

Place chops back in skillet along with the saved mushroom water. Add enough chicken stock so liquid is half way up the sides of the chops. Season with salt and a good pinch of dried rosemary.

Bring to a boil, cover and braise chops in preheated oven for 30 minutes or until tender. You want the chops to simmer in the oven, check after 5 minutes, if the liquid is boiling too rapidly, turn your oven to 325 degrees and continue baking. Remove from oven and transfer chops to a plate and tent with foil. Bring liquid in skillet to a boil and reduce to a thin gravy, adjust seasoning with salt and pepper.

# Mushroom Polenta

*Making polenta at home for dinner, I discovered all I had was Masa Harina which is a fine ground corn flour instead of the traditional coarse ground meal. I discovered a whole new thing. The Polenta was creamy and smooth and didn't take as long to cook. When you are looking for a substitute for mashed potatoes I strongly suggest trying polenta this way.*

2 ½ cups cold water

1 ½ tsp sea salt

1 large clove garlic, minced

Black pepper to taste

2 Tbls chopped fresh parsley

Reserved chopped porcini mushrooms

Just in case you have them on hand, a few sauteed leeks

1 cup Masa Harina

2 Tbls olive oil or butter

Place cold water in a 2 quart sauce pan. Stir in salt, garlic, pepper, parsley, mushrooms and leeks if using. Whisk in Masa Harina until smooth and bring mixture to a boil. Cook polenta, stirring constantly over medium heat until thick and creamy and pulling from the sides of the pot. This should only take about 10 minutes. Stir in oil or butter. Serve immediately with pork chops and pan gravy.

# Apple Crostata with Crystallized Ginger

*A crostata is really just a one crust open faced pie, with the sides folded in to hold the filling. They are quick, easy and open to versatility. I have jazzed this one up a bit with apricot jam and ginger.*

## Crust

1 ½ cups unbleached all purpose flour

1 ½ Tbls sugar

⅓ tsp salt

10 Tbls chilled unsalted butter

3-4 Tbls cold water

Combine the flour, sugar and salt in the bowl of a food processor. Add the butter, cut into small pieces and process until a coarse meal forms. With the machine running add the water and process until dough starts to pull together. Gather into a disk, wrap in plastic and chill for 30 minutes

## Filling

1 ½ pounds fresh apples, peeled, cored and cut into ¼-inch slices. (Use your favorite type of apple, I use a mixture of what I find at the farm stands in the fall)

3 Tbls white sugar

2 Tbls brown sugar

2 Tbls minced crystallzied ginger or more to taste

Juice of ½ lemon

2 Tbls unsalted butter

⅔ cup apricot jam

½ cup toasted walnuts, roughly chopped

2 Tbls cream

Preheat oven to 375 degrees.

Toss apples with sugars, ginger, and lemon juice.

Roll chilled crust out to a 14" circle. Spread bottom of center of crust with apricot jam, leaving a 2-inch space from the edge of the jam to the edge of the crust. Top jam circle with apple mixture. Sprinkle apples with toasted nuts if using. Dot with butter. Fold the 2 inches of plain crust toward the apples, forming an open pocket all the way around. Brush top of crust with cream and sprinkle with sugar.

Bake crostata until crust is golden brown and the apples are tender, about 45 minutes.

Serve warm or at room temperature.

# Mint Fudge Brownies

*I shop at Marden's so often that when the founding owner died people asked me if I was going to his funeral. Marden's is only in Maine, has branches all over the state and carries surplus and salvaged goods.*

*You can find anything from designer clothes to new windows for your house. Most of the dishes from the restaurant have been found by wandering Marden's aisles, along with the fabric for my quilts, the rugs for my rooms and the floor tile in the bathroom. One day I stumbled upon boxes and boxes of mint chocolate chips and couldn't resist. Thankfully I didn't because these brownies are delicious.*

6 ounces unsweetened chocolate, chopped

3 sticks unsalted butter (24 Tbls), softened

1 ¾ cups unbleached all purpose flour

1 ½ tsp baking soda

1 tsp salt

1 cup sugar

1 cup packed brown sugar

4 extra large eggs

3 cups mint chocolate chips

**Makes approximately 24 2-inch brownies**

Preheat the oven to 350 degrees. Grease a 9" x13" baking pan.

Melt unsweetened chocolate and butter in a microwave or double boiler on the stove. Stir until smooth and set aside to cool for 10 minutes.

Meanwhile whisk together the flour, soda and salt in a small bowl.

In a large bowl beat the sugars and eggs until light and fluffy, about 3 minutes. Scrape down the sides of the bowl and add the melted chocolate mixture until combined. Fold in the flour mixture and mint chocolate chips just until blended. Pour batter into the prepared pan and bake for 30 minutes, or until the top is dry and shiny. Don't count on a cake tester because the center will be a bit runny when you pull them from the oven. That is what gives them their fudgy consistency. Let the brownies cool completely before cutting.

I dust them with powdered sugar. These are rich, so you might want to cut them small.

# Quick Bites

## Medjool Dates Stuffed with Cream Cheese

Buy plump dried dates, split them in half and remove the pit. Fill each half with cream cheese. If you feel you need some protein, top each half with an almond.

## Chopped Salad, My Version

1 orange bell pepper, cored, seeded and cut into bite size pieces

½ cucumber, peeled, quartered and sliced

¼ cup Kalamata olives, pitted and chopped

1 Tbls red wine vinegar

3 Tbls really good olive oil

Sprinkle of salt

Put all ingredients in a bowl and mix together. I eat the whole thing as a meal.

In the summer I add fresh tomatoes and a creamy feta for a special treat.

## Perfect Prime Rib

Drizzle roast with olive oil. Sprinkle liberally with kosher salt, black pepper, dry mustard, dried thyme and granulated garlic.

Roast in a 375 degree oven until meat thermometer registers 110 degrees for medium rare, between 45 minutes and an hour and a half depending on the size of your roast.

## Spiced Nuts

1 cup whole nuts, pecans are my favorite

½ tsp cocoa powder

1 tsp five spice powder

½ tsp ancho chili powder

2 tsp date sugar or 1 tsp brown sugar or 1 Tbls maple syrup

Large pinch of chipotle chili powder

1 tsp sea salt or to taste

2 Tbls sunflower oil

Heat oven to 350 degrees. Place nuts in a single layer on a baking tray and toast in oven for 10 minutes, or until golden brown. Combine remaining ingredients in a bowl big enough to accommodate the nuts. Remove nuts from oven and immediately pour into bowl. Toss. Pour out onto a tray and allow to cool completely.

## Greek Yogurt with Fresh Berries

8 ounces Greek Yogurt

1 Tbls maple syrup

1 – 2 cups fresh berries

Mix the maple syrup into the yogurt and pour over berries. Also try Greek yogurt with a bit of fruit jam stirred in. It tastes like ice cream!

Greek yogurt also makes a wonderful savory dip. Add curry and cilantro or caramelized onions, salt and granulated garlic.

## Swordfish Kebabs with Cucumber Yogurt Sauce

1 ½ pounds fresh swordfish, cut into 1 ½ inch chunks

Cherry tomatoes

Chunks of red onion

Marinate fish in ¼ cup lemon juice, ¼ cup white wine, ¼ cup olive oil, 1 tsp cumin, ½ tsp dried oregano or 1 Tbls fresh, salt and pepper to taste.

Make kebabs of fish, cherry tomatoes and red onion. Grill 2 minutes on each side, there are 4 sides to a kebab.

Mix together 1 cup yogurt, ½ cucumber, chopped, a bit of fresh mint or basil and salt and pepper to taste. Serve with kebabs as a dipping sauce.

# More Quick Bites

## Grilled Skirt Steak

*My most favorite thing in the whole world growing up was my Mother's grilled skirt steak.*

1 pound skirt steak
¼ cup olive oil
½ cup red wine
3 cloves of garlic, slivered
Kosher salt
Freshly ground black pepper

Place the steak in a shallow pan. Whisk the oil, wine and garlic together and pour over steak. Cover and refrigerate at least 1 hour and up to 3. Take steak out of fridge 30 minutes before grilling. Season with salt and pepper. Grill 3-4 minutes per side. This steak is best eaten medium rare. It is a very flavorful piece of meat, but can be tough if overcooked.

## Dessert Fruit Canapes

4 slices of a good, heavy, homemade bread
6 Tbls melted unsalted butter
2 Tbls honey
1 Tbls cinnamon
Brie, or other soft cheese
Slices of mango, kiwi, strawberries, pineapple, etc.

**Makes approximately 24 canapes**

Preheat oven to 400 degrees.
Remove crusts from bread and cut into 2-inch squares. Brush with melted butter, honey and cinnamon.
Place coated bread on a baking tray and bake in hot oven for 5-10 minutes or until golden brown, toasted and bubbling. Remove from oven and top each square with a piece of cheese and a slice or two of fruit.
Drizzle with warm jam or Dulce de Leche (caramel sauce).

# Cooking in the Moment — Index of Recipes